S0-ADH-158

CANOEING MAP

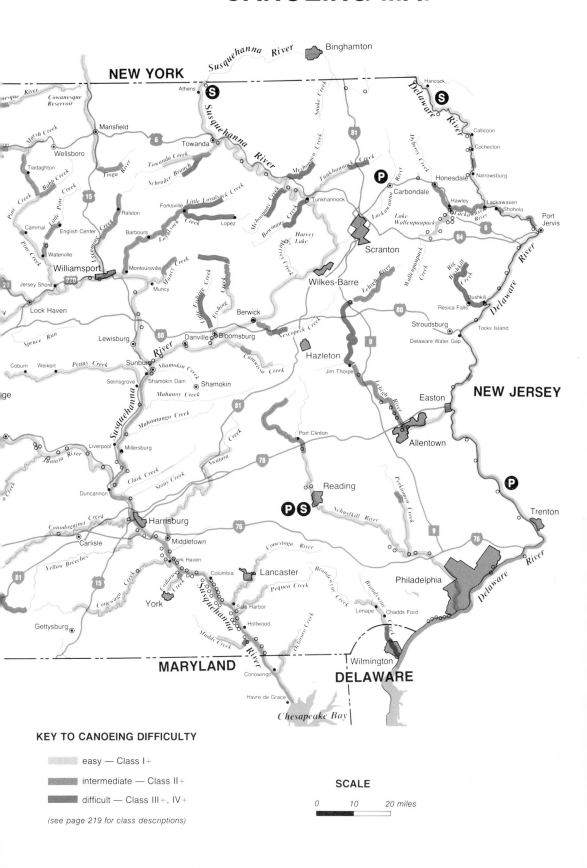

KEY TO CANOEING DIFFICULTY

easy — Class I+

intermediate — Class II+

difficult — Class III+, IV+

(see page 219 for class descriptions)

SCALE

0   10   20 miles

Rivers of Pennsylvania

Rivers
of
Pennsylvania

Tim Palmer

 Keystone Books

The Pennsylvania State University Press

University Park and London

Frontispiece: A mountain tributary to Schrader Branch, Towanda Creek

Parts of several chapters originally appeared in
Wilderness Camping, Trout, Pennsylvania Angler, and
River World

Library of Congress Cataloging in Publication Data

Palmer, Tim.
Rivers of Pennsylvania

(Keystone books)
Includes bibliography.
1. Rivers—Pennsylvania. I. Title.
GB1225.P4P33   917.48'09'693   79-15378
ISBN 0-271-00226-3 cloth
ISBN 0-271-00246-8 paper

for Cindy, who always heard the river's singing

Contents

Acknowledgments

My thanks to many river people: Cindy Palmer, Bob McCullough, Jim McClure, Ed McCarthy, Pete Fletcher, Jerry Walls, Helen Wilhelm, Art Davis, Red Arnold, Ken Sink, John Oliver, Walt Lyon, Bob Cortez, Gerry Lacy, John Sweet, Jerry Miller, Bill Parsons, George Reese, Bob Butler, Cass Chestnut, Bob Banks, Howard Brown and others. Although most photos were taken by me, four are by John Lazenby of Moretown, Vermont, and the historical photos were provided by the Lycoming County Historical Museum. Much of the black and white photo printing was done by Vannucci Photos and Mark Anderman of Williamsport.

Maps at the front and back of the book were prepared by Bob Texter and Chris van Dyck. Base map information was compiled from the *Official Map of Pennsylvania (1977)* prepared by the Pennsylvania Department of Transportation and the *Stream Map of Pennsylvania (1965)* prepared by Howard Wm. Higbee. *Canoeing Map* details were obtained from *Canoeing Guide to Western Pennsylvania and Northern West Virginia* by the Pittsburgh Council of American Youth Hostels, Inc., and from *Appalachian Waters 1: The Delaware and Its Tributaries* and *Appalachian Waters 3: The Susquehanna River and Its Tributaries* by Walter E. Burmeister. Public access, fishery, and acid mine drainage details on the *Fishing Map* were provided by the Pennsylvania Fish Commission.

Introduction: Penn's Rivers

Pennsylvania is a land of rivers and streams, 45,000 miles of them flowing toward the Chesapeake Bay, Delaware estuary, Great Lakes, and Gulf of Mexico. These waters brought European explorers into wilderness of the Indian's land, and later the continent was settled by people who drifted down the Ohio on keelboats. Today, streams twist and foam as they descend rocky, wooded slopes of the Appalachian Plateau. They wind through farmlands in a pastoral way, then roll slowly around cities and lowlands. Adding their increasing volume to one another, they grow in power. The rivers have distinction and importance of many kinds:

95 percent of our domestic water supply comes from rivers and streams. Water of one major river is used seven times before it reaches the sea.

Streams of the north central highlands are the wildest, least developed between New York and Chicago.

In southwestern Pennsylvania, the Youghiogheny provides more whitewater recreation than any other river in the nation.

Pittsburgh is America's busiest inland port. The Ohio River carries more commerce than the Panama Canal.

Legislation in 1978 designated the upper and middle Delaware as a National Scenic and Recreational River. Five other streams are being considered for federal protection.

The Lehigh River, Pine Creek, and the Susquehanna's West Branch have gorges of 1000-foot depth. They are scenic and recreational highlights of the Appalachians.

Bordering the Schuylkill River, Fairmount Park is the country's largest urban greenspace.

Wildlife thrive along many streams. Some of the finest fishing in the East is here. Commercial fishermen of the Chesapeake are dependent on the quality of Susquehanna water.

Other specialties go unrecognized. This book will discuss many of them.

How does one begin to view the vast complex of Pennsylvania waters? We can generalize and see differences between the north and south. Many northern rivers plunge from rapids to pools, crowded by steep slopes of

Opposite: Loyalsock Creek, below route 220, near the Haystacks

hemlock, hardwoods, and pine. Wildness and small towns are both found along the shorelines. While the origin, the paths, and the appearance of many streams are similar, they also reveal unending variety. In the south, some rivers are steep, wild, and rocky, but most form a meandering boundary of fields and communities. Waters become sluggish with dams or vile with waste. Each stream changes constantly, with every bend opening onto a new scene. Each valley is different from the last.

The Susquehanna, Pine Creek, Loyalsock, Moshannon, Juniata, Allegheny, Clarion, Youghiogheny, Lehigh, and Delaware—these rivers have been given separate chapters in this book. Short sketches describe other important waterways: French and Tionesta creeks are well known in western parts of the state. The Casselman has wild whitewater, though acid mine drainage has destroyed its life. The First Fork of the Sinnemahoning attracts crowds of anglers, while the scenic Bennett and Driftwood branches of the same stream are excellent for canoeing. Penns Creek and the Lackawaxen are favorites of trout fishermen, and expert whitewater runners meet Wills Creek, Stony Creek, and the Slippery Rock. The Schuylkill's lower reaches are a rowing center of the nation. In the southeast, the Brandywine flows through gentle, open landscape that faces development pressure. Johnstown's Conemaugh is notorious for floods. The Monongahela is much-used and polluted; the Ohio is a giant in size and industry.

In one book it is impossible to deal with all the waterways of Pennsylvania or with all aspects of their character and use. *Rivers of Pennsylvania* emphasizes the scenic, less-developed rivers of our state. These are the streams most suitable for recreation, and because of their high quality, environmental degradation would represent a great loss. Most chapters focus upon issues of importance, such as scenic river designation, acid mine drainage, recreational use, dam construction, and water pollution.

The overall organization of the book is by major river basins: first the Susquehanna, the largest in Pennsylvania; next the Ohio; and finally the Delaware. Although streams feeding the Potomac, Genesee, and Lake Erie basins also run through small parts of the Keystone State, these waterways are not discussed except for a short sketch of the Potomac's Wills Creek. This follows the sketch of the Ohio basin's Casselman River, which shares the same mountain source near the Mason-Dixon Line.*

As a prologue to other chapters, "The Natural River" describes riverine evolution before people intervened. A concluding chapter, "The Future of Pennsylvania Rivers," summarizes the challenges of environmental protection. Following the formal chapters, a section headed "Information for River People" presents guidelines for safe and satisfying recreational experiences.

---

*A table headed "Major Stream Basins of Pennsylvania" at the back of the book lists all the state's streams with watersheds of one hundred square miles or more, grouped under the five basins.

The Susquehanna Basin

The Susquehanna is our country's largest river basin on the Atlantic coast, and the West Branch is one of the least developed streams of its size in the East. Twenty-four miles of river wind between Karthaus and Keating in a deeply incised valley with mountains that rise 800 and 1,000 feet from the shore. The Susquehanna is many rivers in one. A ten-day voyage will take the canoeist through coal country, a wild canyon, small towns, fertile farmland, the state capital, hydroelectric dams, and finally the coastal plain and Chesapeake Bay. The waterway bisects three major regions of the state: the rugged Appalachian Plateau, the picturesque Ridge and Valley Province, and the rolling Piedmont.

Pine Creek, attracting thousands of fishermen and canoeists, is known for its scenery of mountains and gorges. The "Grand Canyon of Pennsylvania" has been a popular tourist stop for half a century. More than other streams, this one has been the focus of protection activities. The efforts of residents, preservationists, and various levels of government have been intense, sometimes successful, and always instructive in showing the complexity of approaches to river protection—some that have worked and some that have not.

Twenty-five more miles to the east, the Loyalsock empties into the widening West Branch near Williamsport. No river has the dual excellence of this one—superb trout fishing along chilling pools and hemlock-shaded

Photo courtesy of Lycoming County Historical Museum

West Branch of the Susquehanna near Williamsport, 1900-1910

banks, and unsurpassed kayaking or canoeing in the upper reaches. Eastern whitewater championships have been held here, and the annual races at Worlds End State Park attract thousands of contestants and visitors. For those who aren't expert with a paddle, this river offers hiking along the banks, with rapids, cliffs, glacial boulders, and aged timber as highlights.

Moshannon Creek enters the Susquehanna's West Branch above Karthaus, after a tumultuous pitch that is a favorite among whitewater canoeists of central Pennsylvania. Ironically, acid pollution is partly responsible for wild Moshannon shorelines—without game fish, there has been very little pressure for access roads and cabin developments. A proposed dam at Keating would flood the Moshannon, the West Branch Canyon, and two other streams that have been recommended for consideration in the Pennsylvania State Scenic Rivers System.

From the sandstone ridges and limestone valleys of south central Pennsylvania, the Juniata flows slowly eastward. Natural chemistry of the water and reduced pollution have made the Juniata remarkably productive for stream life. Shellfish seem to cover the bottom in places, and crayfish can often be found under large rocks. Great blue herons, green herons, kingfishers, mergansers, and other waterfowl thrive, as do bass and muskellunge and people fishing for them. The food chain and ecosystem of a freshwater stream can be seen here more easily than other places because

Photo courtesy of Lycoming County Historical Museum

Log rafts at the Hepburn Street Dam, Williamsport, 1900

Photo courtesy of Lycoming County Historical Museum

The Hiawatha, near Williamsport, about 1900

aquatic life is so evident. Not all of the Juniata is healthy, though. Wastes from a paper mill radically affect the river's upper reaches; however, improvements in water quality have made the Juniata famous as a "comeback" stream, one where abatement of pollution has made a difference.

Several of Pennsylvania's rivers were critical to the history of our country. William Penn settled the lower Delaware, and at the Ohio River's origin, Fort Duquesne, or Fort Pitt, was an important frontier outpost of the French and Indian War. Canal systems paralleled many large waterways. The history of the upper Susquehanna is especially interesting, for it was by this river that Pennsylvania's great but unknown explorer, Etienne Brulé, crossed the state in 1615 and 1616. One hundred fifty years later, the valley housed a core of pioneering settlements, and here the Iroquois Nations tried to reclaim their lands during the Revolutionary War.

The Ohio Basin

The Ohio is the state's second largest river basin. Here the broad and well-known Allegheny captures and carries most of the rainfall from northwestern Pennsylvania. Scenic reaches from Buckaloons to Oil City and from Franklin to Emlenton are very popular, serving as an unspoiled recreation area for the industrialized regions of Pittsburgh, Erie, and eastern Ohio.

Above the town of Warren lies Kinzua Dam and a thirty-mile-long reservoir that was built in 1967, displacing people of the Seneca Nation of Indians. Efforts of the Western Pennsylvania Conservancy, state government, and the United States Forest Service have been effective in protecting some of the Allegheny islands and shorelines below Warren. The lower river is dammed for commercial river traffic, and shorelines are often developed. Valued because of their scarcity, some open spaces are being protected and opened for public access to the water.

The Clarion is one of the Allegheny's largest tributaries, wild and scenic as it penetrates the mountains. Below Portland Mills and again below Cooksburg, there are no paralleling roads or railroads, only rhododendron-lined banks that rise sharply to steep slopes. The Allegheny National Forest, state forests, game lands, and parks adjoin the river, one-fourth of the shoreline being in public ownership. The lower twenty miles includes one of the wildest sections, though it shows clear evidence of problems. Acid mine drainage is severe in this reach, as it is on many tributaries. Piney Dam impounds the river for twelve miles near the town of Clarion, and a new dam that would inundate thirty miles of river has been proposed at St. Petersburg, five miles above the Allegheny. Sewage and industrial wastes have severely polluted the stream; however, recent years have brought improvements in nearly all aspects of water quality. A 1971 report of the Federal Bureau of Outdoor Recreation recommended that the Clarion not be designated in the National Wild and Scenic Rivers System, but suggested that it be reconsidered when water quality improves.

Southwestern Pennsylvania has the incomparable Youghiogheny, the finest of the whitewater streams. With a rare combination of clarity, wildness, challenging rapids, and accessibility, this is one of the most floated rivers in the world. One hundred thousand rafters, canoeists, and kayakers splash through Youghiogheny turbulence each year. The contrast of dark forests and brilliant churning water cannot be found elsewhere in the state. Outfitters serve masses of people with astonishing safety: there have been no drownings among guided groups. River running is a new phenomenon, and in the last ten years, this sport, and a state park, have transformed the quiet mountain town of Ohiopyle to a busy recreation center.

Opposite: Sunrise, Susquehanna above New Buffalo

The Delaware Basin

In the east, the Delaware basin incorporates unusual variety. Wildwater pours from the Pocono plateau, and much of it falls toward the sea by way of the Lehigh River. Below Walters Dam, rafters and kayakers converge on the third weekend of each month as extra water is released from the impoundment, guaranteeing a rapid journey through a spectacular gorge to the town of Jim Thorpe. Fishermen also like the Lehigh, and boater-angler conflicts are becoming common here, as they are on some other rivers. The Lehigh is being considered for inclusion in Pennsylvania's Scenic Rivers System.

A master of rivers, the Delaware is outstanding in many ways. Its history involves some of the earliest settlers on the continent, and its estuary is a major seaport. Above Trenton, the river's ecosystem is one of diversity and vigor, with fish, birds, mammals, and plant life to fascinate the naturalist. The Delaware has more recreational use than many other rivers combined, as a nature-starved urban population flocks to the upper reaches which became Pennsylvania's first National River in 1978. Headwaters provide drinking water to New York City.

Growing Importance of Rivers

In the past people have relied upon waterways as a means of transportation and as a source of water, fish, or power. The added importance of rivers in the future cannot be overestimated. A movement is under way that represents a definite and complex trend. Though there has been no clear focus, it involves rivers as the center of many approaches in recreational activity, environmental protection, and land-use planning. Several features of the trend are apparent:

Emphasis has been given to wild, scenic, and recreational river programs at the national and at some state levels. In the past eight years, eighty-three streams of the United States have been nominated for or included in a national system, and twenty-seven states have begun scenic-river programs of their own.*

The Clean Streams Act of Pennsylvania and the Federal Water Pollution Control Act have been effective instruments toward elimination of pollution. Much remains to be done.

---

*A table at the back of the book lists the streams recommended for study by the Scenic Rivers Task Force, Pennsylvania Department of Environmental Resources. Streams are located by basin and by county.

High construction costs, resistance to land acquisition, and expenses of facility operation mean less likelihood of major new park developments. Recreation will become more common in "open systems" that involve a mixture of public and private land with an emphasis on natural area appeal—conditions that are found along many rivers.

Due to a scarcity of suitable sites, high costs, social-environmental impacts, and a frequent surplus of reservoir recreation areas, fewer dams are likely to be built in the future. Rivers, rather than man-made lakes, will answer many of our water-related needs. Counter to this trend is the water-resource development philosophy of some public agencies, concern for electric power production, local pressures for flood control, and the possibility of future water shortages.

Nearly every community has a stream flowing past it. Leisure-time opportunities can be available close to home, without traveling great distances.

Rivers as a means of recreational travel are increasing greatly in popularity. People are discovering that a whole network of wilderness "highways" can be explored.

Flood-plain management is recognized in many areas as a priority concern that can economically lead to decreased flood damages and to open space protection of stream frontage. In the larger sense, a "natural systems approach" toward land-use planning, which recognizes ecological and social values of the riverine environment, is being instituted in many places.

The future poses many questions about the rivers of Pennsylvania—questions that will involve the welfare of people who live there, the concerns of visitors who enjoy the waters, and the interest of those who simply admire a river and its life. Problems are present. Pollution and flood-plain development threaten the valuable qualities of many waterways. Downstream needs for water supply, flood control, and electric power generation will lead to more pressure for dams. With many conflicting goals for our streams, we need various means to meet a variety of objectives. In making difficult decisions regarding the future of Pennsylvania rivers, an understanding of the resource is important. It is hoped that this book will help us toward a better knowledge of our rivers and their meaning in our lives.

Page 10: Brandywine Creek above Lenape

Page 11: Lehigh River above Oxbow Bend

The Natural River

Where forests, farms, and towns can now be seen, waters once gleamed as a mirror through the day, or at night, the wind-tossed waves reflected the brilliance of a full moon. Today's highlands of northern Pennsylvania were a vast sea of prehistoric water, while the human race was yet unborn.

These waters of 400 million years ago were surrounded by higher ground, and the continuing cycle of evaporation, condensation, and rainfall brought another continuing but markedly slower cycle to the region now known as the Appalachian Plateau. This was the unending flow of silt and sand from land to the water. For eons it continued, layer upon layer of earth settling beneath currents and waves, burdening the floor of the ancient Pennsylvanian sea. Under the added pressure of this mighty deposit, the inner earth became heated, accumulating energy for a process of massive change.

Pressure within the earth at last reached a cataclysmic level, and the planet's crusted surface could sustain no more. The upheaval began, and once again, the earth that had been water-borne, as minute particles of soil, returned toward the sky and the open air from which it came. Underwater

West Branch Susquehanna below Montoursville

depths gave way, in this upheaval of 200 million years ago, and the northern sea of the Appalachians slowly flowed from its rising floor, channeling
new routes to a lower level as waters receded. The land rose higher and
higher; subterranean pressure was unceasing in its release of energy. A
cycle had been completed: mountains to the sea and then to high plateau
again. Evidence of the plateau can be seen from hundreds of overlooks
across northern Pennsylvania—high ridges that are almost level and uni-
form in their elevation.

Change is unending, and the flattened mass of the Appalachian Plateau
began to age. Soils of earlier erosion had consolidated into rock under
waters that screened out the daylight; now the process reversed itself, as
the hard surface loosened and softened into soil that could support a host
of plant life in the millenia that lay ahead. Prehistoric rains pounded new
clay from shale and sand from stone, and waters rinsed away the lightest
fragments, carrying them downward on a new journey to a distant ocean.
Forces of water wore upon the highlands, just as they do today.

In this way the rivers of northern Pennsylvania were born. From an almost indeterminate slope, they began their descent across the plateau,
weaving most often from north to south. We think of rivers as beginning
where the highest rainfall lands and following a well-defined route to the
sea; instead, the channels and stream valleys evolved from the lowest point
upward. Where a rill or drainage course formed, waters constantly washed
soil away to make the channel deeper. As they did so, the water-carving
action would also extend upstream, with floods and heavy runoff plucking
particles of earth from headwater regions and rinsing them downward.
The most erodible upland soils and rocks were the first to become dis-
lodged, and the network of streams advanced upward following a crooked
route of least resistance. Thus the many-fingered paths of the Delaware,
Susquehanna, and Allegheny penetrated a plateau, and sculptured artwork
of rivers infiltrated all corners of the highlands.

In later years people would gaze up in wonder at rugged slopes rising
from the canyon of the Susquehanna's West Branch and other places.
From the river, the depth of the eroded trough makes the plateau *seem* like
a range of pointed or folded peaks. In fact, valleys were carved out rather
than the mountains built up.

Rivers sway from side to side, sometimes pounding a shoreline or rocky
cliff, but usually rolling over the stream bed and gently slicking the earth at
its edge. Dislocated soil is carried downstream, leaving clean riverstone and
bedrock behind. While the lightest silt does not hesitate on its journey to
the Gulf of Mexico, the Delaware estuary, or the Chesapeake Bay, larger
particles of earth do. They settle wherever the water slows, at quiet pools
or on the inside of great bends, brown fragments swirling in eddies at the
edge of a rapid current. Sand and gravel bars are thus formed, and islands
appear where the current pursues two routes downhill.

Page 14: Clarion River at Cook Forest

Page 15: Loyalsock Creek above Barbours

During floods, the washing of soil is accelerated a thousand times or even ten thousand times. Then the rivers sweep land away in a process that has continued since the rising of the plateau, a process that created the scenic grandeur of northern Pennsylvania valleys and gorges. When the high flow overtops its banks, muddied waters become ponded on the flood plain, and the grains of suspended soil settle once again to the ground. Countless times this has been repeated, leaving broad and flat expanses of flood-borne silt, finely textured and rich in fertility. This is the lush agricultural plain of nearly all large rivers.

No process of building occurs without the destruction of something else, and so, while flood plains are being developed in one place, they are disappearing in others—the river turns upon lands it created, washing them into the current again, to be redeposited elsewhere downstream. The waterway continually changes its course. Belatedly, people have realized this as homes crash into the channel of a raging flood, the wandering current having undermined a cinder-block foundation. The river leaves its ancient channels only temporarily.

As the rivers worked deep into the plateau of northern Pennsylvania, higher lands crumbled and weathered into a surface that could hold moisture between fine particles. When the moisture froze, its volume expanded, bursting and further fracturing the earthen crust. Life took hold as lichens grasped onto stone. The process of birth and growth developed in a spartan but nourishing environment. Death and decay followed; life was breeding on life, and the surface of the plateau took on a darker, softer complexion. Roots and humus of new ages settled and tangled with finer particles of soil, and a cycle of increased fertility and greater growth began. This pattern was to continue uninterrupted until a disastrous stripping of vegetation left the soil bare. In 1880 the towering trees of centuries were cut for cities and railroad ties of a growing America, and the humus of ages was seared or destroyed by fires that raged over millions of acres on the Appalachian Plateau.

When the first Europeans set foot on the American Continent and began to clear and plow their way inland from the sea, a wilderness engulfed northern Pennsylvania. Then as now, the dominant features were rivers, which bound the region together in a branching pattern of life. Columns of conifers grew interspaced with giant hardwoods—ash, maple, beech, oak, basswood, poplar, and others. With enclosing shade, small streams seldom heated beyond the groundwater temperature of fifty-five degrees. Soil was a matted duff, full of decomposing vegetation and forest-floor organisms. It held water like a sponge, retaining the snowmelt and rains, then releasing pure water slowly. As a result, a mature pine log could float the length of Pine Creek during the summer. Today, without the softer, absorbing forest floor of the past, water speeds to the Chesapeake much faster, leaving a rocky stream bed in the dryness of August.

At the water's edge three distinct ecosystems existed. The deepest shade and quiet shelter of the forest met the sunlight of the flood plain and the aquatic life of flowing water. Tangled, impenetrable masses of willow, witch hazel, and birch thrived along the banks. They were a full-course meal for the beaver, but the aspen that grew in the sunshine was its favorite. Swallows nested in the eroding sand banks, and mallards ate from the shallows, while herons waded in open flats of warm, ponded water. Mergansers dove in deeper pools, with the osprey and eagle competing for cold and warm water fishes. Like the salmon of New England, shad migrated to headwaters each year, their backs rolling to the surface as they powerfully pushed their way upward on a journey for survival of their species—something that hasn't happened on many streams since the first Susquehanna dam was built. Elk roamed in herds along some northern rivers. They lumbered to a wild shoreline in the evening, their darkened skins and bleached antlers majestic on the glistening riffles, a sight no one sees today.

Page 18: Lower Moshannon Creek

Page 19: Moshannon Creek below route 53

Photo courtesy of Lycoming County Historical Museum

Log jam, West Branch of the Susquehanna at Curwensville, 1900

Beyond the gravel bars grew the yellow birch, crowded together with their peeling papery skins and newer branches showing red tips in the sun. Then came the sycamores, giants of the riverine ecosystem. They had trunks of two, three, and four feet across, roots probing into the water beneath the alluvial soil, and branches of white, tan, and olive designs where old bark would peel and fall, showing a new and different surface beneath.

At the edge of water and land, forest and brush, most dramas of the wilderness were played. While primeval shade was welcome cover, the river's edge meant food. Not only was the slapping-tailed beaver attracted to the tender shoots and brushy landscape, but the muskrat built its home of sticks and mud here. Mink passed silently through wooded sections, and otter sneaked and slid along deep pools. Animals that preferred the forest came to the edge intermittently. On a log that protruded into the current, a raccoon would crouch to moisten its food each night. The bobcat was found, and occasionally the lynx, for these streams carry a dual identity, one of the north and one of the south.

Plant life reflects both these elements. Red pine can be found here, a northern tree. Virginia pines, native to a warmer land, stand in scattered groups. The sugar maple, hemlock, and beech that characterize New England forests do well on cooler slopes and northern exposure, while the oak and hickory forests that are the mainstay of the Virginia and Carolina Appalachians are also very common. You can find a sassafras in the sun and a balsam fir in secluded shade of a high bog.

The climatic differences that cause the diverse blending of plant life are accentuated by the steep descent from plateau to river bottom—a pattern of topography that is prevalent on many north central rivers, like the Sinnemahoning, Pine Creek, and Loyalsock. While frigid air and northerly winter winds bite and rage on the heights, valleys of five hundred or one thousand feet below lie in comparative mildness. Another effect of the elevation differences is a lowland fog and morning mist occurring almost daily in the summertime. Unable to rise and unable to diffuse itself, moisture-laden air shrouds the narrow valleys until a higher sun can penetrate.

The north central highlands

A picture of these untouched rivers could not be painted today. The vast wilderness that thrived on itself cannot be imagined by people who have seen only a woodlot of virgin timber. Some parks have fortunately been preserved so we may see the forest heritage of Pennsylvania, but they stand more as popular museums, only hints of the immense wilds and forever-winding waters that once flourished here. Primitive and rugged high country of some western states has been preserved, but it cannot compare to the fertile richness of the darkened forest floor and the gently glimmering brilliance of northern Pennsylvania rivers only two hundred years ago.

A character is left, however, and wherever rivers flow free we can see a part of these earlier waterways. Because of their scarcity, the wildest reaches have become invaluable as samples and relics of the riverine environment that Indians joined and that early explorers and settlers faced.

The rivers of Pennsylvania include these reminders and more. Their shorelines are now traveled by railroads. Coal formed in ancient ages is mined from the plateau. Communities stand on flood plains and high banks. Dams have put an end to some parts of the rivers, flattening their flow for miles. What is a river of Pennsylvania like today? Let's take a look.

Opposite: Bear Run, tributary to Pine Creek

The Susquehanna Basin

A River Voyage:
The Susquehanna and Its West Branch

Through a mist not yet touched by early sunlight, we began the journey. The world ahead of us lay obscured; it seemed two-dimensional, with depth missing. We listened to the rush of flowing water, then peered into grayness that seemed prehistoric, like artists' drawings of the first day that amphibian creatures became reptiles and stepped forth onto a steaming rocky landscape. Water swirled and the air grew patchy, so that we could see through voids to a wooded shoreline of dripping hemlocks and shining rhododendron. Rivers are mysterious, but never more so than in fog. Each stroke of the paddle, each instant of movement brought another discovery, a rock to miss, a merganser moving away from us. Distant scenes gradually became recognizable, like an image through binoculars that are slowly being focused.

On this trip there were four of us, in two canoes, my wife Cindy and I in one, Bob and Marna Banks in the other. This wasn't my first journey down the West Branch of the Susquehanna, but somehow, the experience always seems new. For a while, I thought the feeling was caused by seeing different things and by paddling alternate routes. The changing seasons, weather, and wildlife make each cruise unique. Later I realized that the water itself, so foreign to our landlocked lives, makes every voyage new and exciting. Some of us can swim across the English Channel or the Susquehanna River, but we are still land creatures. Though water is common to us, it is mysterious, ephemeral, evaporating into the sky, then falling again out of nowhere. The greatest thrill is the motion. On land, only *we* move, but on rivers, we move *and* our highway moves. To deal with both-as-one is an art. Those who travel rivers often use the phrase "reading the water." It means to know what the stream is doing and what it will do to *you*. And so, during those first few minutes, the solid tie to land is broken and the tenuous relationship to water is established. Ready or not, travel begins as the current clutches its new partner, and we are off on a journey to the sea.

Opposite: Sterling Run in the West Branch Canyon

Canoeing on the upper West Branch

This river is one of four in northern Pennsylvania that have sufficient flow for a summer voyage. All are worth traveling, but the upper West Branch is a favorite. Unlike the Delaware and Allegheny, both branches of the Susquehanna can easily be followed to salt water. This ambition is complicated by days of polluted tidal flow on the Delaware and by 2,000 miles of flat and dirty current below the Allegheny. Mountains of the West Branch are continuously higher and the shoreline is wilder than nearly any river of its size in Pennsylvania. Sometimes the midsummer flow is too sparse for rockless canoeing, but this time we had high and fast water from our starting point below Shawville.

At Moshannon Falls the pace of the river became swift. I thought of the time near Rolling Stone when we met an adventuresome crew who asked, "What happens if you go over the falls?" Cindy explained that if you go over the falls you won't know it, that in fact it's only a small rapids. We splashed our way through, the spray of the river feeling good now that the morning was warm. Below the "falls" the West Branch is joined by Moshannon Creek, a turbulent stream whose bed is stained deep orange from years of acid mine drainage but which still holds values of scenery, wildness, and challenging rapids.

Another hour of drifting took us to Karthaus, a typical Pennsylvania coal town. Deep miners went to stripping long ago, scraping the hills for veins near the top. Coal dust and ordinary dust have left their mark on the village and countryside. Still we are glad to be here, for Karthaus is at the head of the West Branch Canyon, a section of the river with vast complexes of ridge lines, ravines, and shadows. Forming a rugged gorge, layers of forested mountains are seemingly set one upon another as winding waters unfold view after towering view. The pools were as clear as fine crystal, but there were no game fish because of the low pH from acid-bearing shales at the mines. It would be like expecting a trout to live in a cup of coffee.

At Buttermilk Rapids, Cindy and I drew our canoe into swirls and back channels just for the fun of it, while Bob and Marna followed, cutting behind one rock and then around another, always plotting to go somewhere just a little more exciting than the Susquehanna would normally send us. By now it was early afternoon, so at the cool, shaded mouth of Sterling Run, we stopped for lunch and felt like staying a week.

It was sheer summer pleasure as we swam and drifted, Cindy and I in our 16½-foot Mad River canoe and Bob and Marna in a 17-foot Grumman that we borrowed from Ed McCarthy, who outfits and guides canoeists and rafters through Pine Creek Canyon. Earlier in the year I had paddled my smaller 13-foot canoe next to weather-beaten, canyon-molded Ed, age sixty-seven. I told him of our plans for a long journey to the Chesapeake. Interrupting me with his usual enthusiasm, Ed said, "Tim, take this craft; she's a doll in heavy waters. You can load five hundred pounds with room for a Strauss waltz, and a mighty headwind won't send you back to Williamsport, Jersey Shore, Lock Haven." A wrinkled smile broke across his suntanned face. "In your small boat, you'd run as scared as a pregnant fox!" McCarthy himself is unrepeatable and inseparable from the twenty-three miles of water he calls home. His wary stare downstream, his forceful paddle in the muddy crosscurrents of swollen springtime floods, and his mad exuberance on a day when the sun shines set him apart as a personality in a time when most people seem pretty much the same.

Like the canyon that Ed runs, this section of river is an outstanding example of Appalachian water. Spruce Run, Burns Run, Yost Run, and a dozen others fall off the mountainsides, unspoiled by rusted signs of acid mine drainage that are so prevalent in the upper basins of many central and western Pennsylvania streams. Valley walls enclose you in a world shared only with friends and a railroad, and good camp sites are plentiful.

The height of mountains increases as you follow the river north from Karthaus. Rocky cliffs hang above Bougher Run, and Twin Hollows form a complex backdrop. Scenery is most spectacular near Yost Run, where ridge lines are 900 feet above, and the gentle current of the river weaves against one shoreline, then the other, an ageless but changing pattern as waters of the highlands fall to the sea. This is the site of the proposed Keating Dam, a project identified by the Army Corps of Engineers in 1934. In 1977 it was reevaluated, but not recommended for construction. With political pressure, however, the project could threaten to permanently flood the West Branch Canyon.

Burnt hashbrowns and overdone eggs tasted delicious in the morning. When you're camping and therefore hungry, you don't even notice, except that the food is a little blacker than it ought to be. A slight stiffness from yesterday and from the chill air of a restful night made us ready for a hot cup of coffee or tea and the savory, smoky taste of anything that will fit in the frying pan. When I eat finely prepared food, I often reflect a little and wish I could enjoy it as much as I enjoy burnt potatoes on a riverbank.

Our expedition of four plus dogs slipped into the water, drifted a moment, then felt the grip of the current. The character of the West Branch changes dramatically at Keating where the Sinnemahoning joins to form a larger river that bends eastward. Renovo marks yet a greater difference. Strip mines, roads, and cabins we had seen, but here the first sizable town of the voyage meets the stream, stark and unpolished. The confines of rugged mountain and narrow valley push buildings to the edge.

Hyner Mountain has a high and curiously capped summit overlooking the West Branch Valley, and on a gravel beach within sight of the peak we

West Branch Susquehanna below Renovo

stopped for lunch. The first canoe of the day came in sight around an upstream bend; looking closely, we saw it carried three boys, probably high school age or so. All three pulled hard on their paddles, forcing the fifteen-foot overloaded boat to surge, then sink. The gunwales or sides of the canoe would rock as the load shifted this way, then that, each time narrowly escaping the river. The three canoeists, wearing swimming trunks, shouted hello. We were soon behind them, drifting into McCloskey Island riffles, one of the better rapids on that part of the Susquehanna. As if in slow motion replay, the canoe shipped one wave over the side, then another. In rapid succession, despite desperate squirming, the boys fell out as the craft rolled. It was no tragedy, so my first concern was to get some good pictures.

"Pull up there where those life jackets are floating, Bob," I shouted. As he deftly swung across the whitewater, snatching stray life jackets from the waves and returning them, I shot film. Cindy backpaddled effectively, keeping our boat in flatter waters. At the instant of lost balance, when the canoe had capsized, I caught a glimpse of beer cans flashing in the sun and then gone to the waves. Rendezvousing with Bob and Marna below the island, I saw them again—on the bottom of their canoe.

"My conscience just wouldn't let me give them back," Bob said, pointing to the two six-packs. "Without all that extra weight they'd have made it through that riff, and next time they're just liable to drown."

Finding a place to sleep that night was a problem. Between Hyner and Lock Haven, the river offers few sites. With the road to the south and railroad to the north, we had our choice of cars, trains, or cabins. Choosing none of them, I scouted a few likely looking areas, only to find a maze of eight-foot-high undergrowth and poison ivy—a sweating haven for mosquitoes. By unexplainable luck, Bob struck upon a spot used by other campers. There we beached, cooked, and enjoyed the sunset.

Early in the still mist of Saturday morning, our canoes rippled quietly through the two-mile pool of Lock Haven Dam where motorboats were docked along the river's edge. We moved forward with caution, as one must when nearing water-over-the-top impoundments. The trouble is that very little can be seen or heard from above. Structures are invisible. A smooth sheet of water slips over the breast of the dam with no riffle but with alarming velocity and force. An anarchy of eddies and whirlpools froth and foam below, all of which are screened from the boater's view. A roar uncommon to the Susquehanna drowns out voices below the dam, but above and on the approach, the sound of falling waters is a muted and seemingly distant warning. After portaging the dam, we began a forty-mile section that parallels Bald Eagle Mountain, the northernmost of high central Pennsylvania ridges.

Even though the water above Lock Haven had an acid content from coal mining that rendered the river unfit for most fish, it was still remarkably clear. The channel would run dark and blue, a submerged paddle blade showing wooden grain in distinct detail. Then, suddenly and soundlessly, the yellow-brown volume of Bald Eagle Creek met the larger stream. It was the end of clear water for the voyage. We could see the silt and waste-laden current along the southern shore, and at the mix line where Bald Eagle met West Branch, it was like pouring cream into coffee. Mud clung together in lacy fingers, penetrating the river, then flowed downhill in a mildly agitated mixture, soon diffusing throughout the water. Though the river was of much greater volume than the creek, the color of suspended earth soon took over the entire waterway with little apparent mutation or dilution. We remembered the thunder and lightning that had driven us off the river on the second night, and the ominous storm clouds that billowed in the southern sky that evening. The Bald Eagle basin had been hit by a summer storm, and now we saw the results. Much of the limestone valley is farmland, a major source of silt in heavy rains, and extensive highway construction was under way for the "Susquehanna Beltway," involving both sides and the stream bed of Fishing Creek, a major tributary.

Worse than mud, Kepone and Mirex have been found in the fish of Spring Creek, another Bald Eagle tributary that flows past State College and through Bellefonte. Caught near the Ruetgers-Nease Chemical Company, the fish showed concentrations of toxic chemicals exceeding United States Food and Drug Administration safety levels. Spring Creek is regarded as one of our better trout streams, and many anglers have been to Fisherman's Paradise, near Bellefonte. The Fish Commission has posted the area most-affected by Ruetgers-Nease, warning people not to eat the fish. The Department of Environmental Resources is suing the company to clean up their old waste lagoons, which are percolating into groundwater and the creek. Bulk dumping of Kepone into Virginia's James River brought public outrage in the mid 1970s, when it was learned that the chemical's caustic effects may last for one hundred years or more, contaminating Chesapeake Bay seafood whenever rough waters stir the poisoned sludge from the James River bed.

After stopping for supplies in Jersey Shore, we fell into a new rhythm of paddling that quickly took us to the Crane Island riffles. For the first time since above Lock Haven, the West Branch narrowed into a swift and tumbling chute. Now, carrying the additional loads of Bald Eagle Creek, Pine Creek, and many lesser streams, the river rolled with a new force. A quiet but relentless pressure engulfed us as the great volume of swollen and muddied waters pushed from behind, swept underneath, and crested in three-foot rollers at both sides.

In dramatic contrast, the riffle ends at the Williamsport stillwater. Impounded by the low dam eleven miles downstream, the Susquehanna quickly settles to a flattened surface. Now that stillness was broken by the sound of motorboats, waterskiers, houseboats, and fishingboats. They

West Branch Susquehanna below Jersey Shore

ripped, roared, putt-putted, and choked. Some gave us the courtesy of slowing or keeping a distance to reduce their wake, and some didn't. We passed the first proliferation of riverfront trailers—mostly replacements from flood destruction in 1972. Many were bought with so-called disaster relief funds—money intended for needy flood victims but also used to put new weekend trailers back on the flood plain where they will be damaged again.

Crawling like ants over the Linden railroad bridge, boys were scaling the stone pier, sitting on a side rail, and climbing iron trusses to the very top. After staring for long moments into the waves, they would leap to enthralling dives from the steel girders. Standing by as backstage actors, silhouetted against the late afternoon sun, younger kids watched and awaited more courage.

Squatter's Island, as it is called, is a long and slender haven of wildness in the city of Williamsport. Here we landed and found a welcoming sign of the Department of Environmental Resources, saying that overnight camping was permitted. Amid ancient remains of stone cribbing that held the 1880 log boom of Williamsport in place, the island had been covered with squatter shacks of canvas or wooden construction. The Hurricane Agnes flood of 1972 swept them all away, and the Department has prohibited development on the state-owned land. It's now a paradise for the modern-day Huck Finn—an excitement of aged willows with rope swings, grapevines, forest, and wildflowers. But Huck wasn't there, and we had the place

Diving from the Linden railroad bridge

to ourselves. Ghostly remains of a trailer lay with one end on the ground and the other wedged high between two trees, its savagely battered hulk pointing to the sky. Amid solitude, songbirds, and low evening sunlight, this former home served as a torn reminder of a river's force.

The next day at seven o'clock, in a sullen mist, we beached and unloaded for portage around the Williamsport Dam. Water was high and swirling below the spillway. We carried around the newly repaired impoundment, stopping long enough to see an angler pull in and gently return a ten-inch bass. The Susquehanna at Williamsport has been making a healthy come-back since the last major acid slug from the Barnes and Tucker mine in 1970. Walleye fishing is excellent, and brown trout have been caught. To chance the chaos of water below the dam would have likely ended in swamped and overturned canoes, so knee deep we waded the boats through a maze of boulders, willows, and snagged driftwood that is usually above water.

Loyalsock Creek entered the river over a broad, sweeping gravel bar at Montoursville. Its crystal clear, shining northern waters met the yellowed current from the south and west. We stared down at gravel five feet below, then plunged headlong into the last clean tributary of notable size on the entire river. All the others were moribund in comparison, lacking the chilling exuberance of that beautiful stream.

The Susquehanna between Montoursville and Muncy has many distinctive features. Leaving the Loyalsock, we knifed our canoes through a riffle, barely fitting between rocks in a small chute. Nothing has been built in the eight-mile section except one cabin and the railroad. Among large rivers, this is one of the most significant undeveloped reaches in Pennsylvania. I thought of a trip we took in April when we saw four ospreys, four mergansers, three wood ducks, two scaups, two grebes, and a ring-billed gull. They were just passing through, headed north, but we also saw the kingfisher, the great blue heron, six mallards, three deer, one muskrat, and a host of more common wildlife that live along the river year round.

Always there are riffles at the islands—Birch, Racetrack, King, and Brock, and water levels continually change them. In high flows, large waves roll through the main channel to the south of the islands, while remote and tree-lined passages to the north may be open for the cautious canoeist. Lower water means the small passages are closed. Rocks and logs become

West Branch Susquehanna at Loyalsock Creek

The West Branch below Montoursville

obstacles that were buried before. We took the south side of Racetrack Island, picking our way with special care through a channel that was riddled with stumps and drowned sycamore trees. If caution is used, it doesn't take a great deal of experience to float the wild reach, but even for those who have piloted hundreds of miles, the size of the Susquehanna gives its own exciting sensation. It's a lot of water for those who are accustomed to smaller streams.

This was our day of big mileage. Paddling at a steady pace, we comfortably passed Muncy at noon, Montgomery at 1:30, then Watsontown, Milton, and Lewisburg in turn. Between the twin bridges of Interstate 80 swam a gang of kids, dwarfed by monolithic structures of concrete and steel. Their shouts were drowned out by truck traffic over the bridge, and I thought, "Somehow, something's gone from the old swimming hole." Lewisburg's church spires are traditional landmarks, marking the approach to that town from far upstream. We stopped there at suppertime, relaxed in the borough's park atop a high bank, and cooked dinner on a public fireplace.

Blue Mountain glowed in the sunset as we neared Northumberland and
Sunbury. A golden sky behind us reflected soft, mellow ripples for a sooth-
ing and relaxing forty-fifth mile of the day. That was our fifth night out,
and suddenly it was a different river where we slept, as the West Branch
met the Main Branch. We had a feeling for the changes, the rhythm, the
life of northern Pennsylvania waters. With their beauty we found ugliness,
with wildness, civilization, and with peacefulness, we'd found excitement,
an energetic happiness. Sunburnt and weathered, we felt as though we belonged. We couldn't imagine doing anything else tomorrow but pulling a
canoe down a massive and widening river. A wary eye downstream was
now second nature, and a long sweep of the paddle—one every other second—had grown to be a habit and a love. It was as though we could go on
forever to a new sunrise, a different land to see, and always a new day to
explore. Mountain rivers have haunted me since. The bend that splashes or
shimmers out of sight is the one where life goes on all the rivers of Pennsylvania.

The Susquehanna at the Penns Creek confluence

Just as a wild, disordered topography marks the Susquehanna valley in its northern and western reaches, so do the graceful, picturesque ridges of central Pennsylvania leave an image of their own. Bald Eagle was the first of the central mountains and one of the most classic in the state. Beginning far to the west, the borderline ridge looms over the river for forty miles and ends at Muncy. Borderline, I say, because this mountain marks the start of the Ridge and Valley Region, a series of high, scenic ridges interspersed with rolling, fertile valleys of limestone farms and meadows. Blue Mountain at Sunbury, Little Mountain below Selinsgrove, Hooflander at Dalmatia, Mahantango at Liverpool, Berry at Millersburg, Peters Cove at Duncannon, Second Mountain at Dauphin, and another Blue Mountain at Harrisburg—all are landmarks to the heartland of Pennsylvania. Unlike the continual folding and winding of the highlands, these are singular and shapely, standing alone to be admired from a distance. South of those peaks we would bisect the gentle and rolling piedmont, and finally, below the Conowingo Dam would be coastal plain and tidewater.

We rose early from beneath the railroad bridge where we'd slept. Nightmares of freight trains didn't compare to the grisly scene of water we faced. As we approached the night before, we sensed a change, but now, in the hazy reflection of dawn, we saw the nauseating brown-yellow chunks of foam and unusually thick particles of solids. Outdoing Bald Eagle Creek, the upper Susquehanna, or North Branch, waters assumed distinction as the ugliest of the trip. Like Bald Eagle, the North Branch experienced heavy rains several days before, which caused the water to look worse than usual.

The first order of business was to move ourselves to the western side of the river, into better-looking water. The two Susquehanna branches remained discrete to Harrisburg and beyond—over fifty miles. Dark brown waters of the North Branch flowed down the eastern side, and lighter waters of the West Branch stayed along that shore.

For our third portage, we landed our canoes next to the Sunbury Fabridam, an inflated fabric dam. State park personnel were scuba diving for missing park property, thought to have been thrown into the river by vandals. Neither the divers nor the crowd of catfish, carp, and bass fishermen had any luck.

With a deep-pitched resonance and a belch of smoke, a new kind of landmark appeared: the electric power plant. The Pennsylvania Power and Light Company's facility at Shamokin Dam was the first of many; we'd see them again at Three Mile Island, York Haven, Brunner Island, Safe Harbor, Holtwood, Peach Bottom, and Conowingo (Maryland). They would become the dominant feature of the river below Harrisburg; this one was just a forerunner.

That afternoon was a squelcher. Sunburnt and sweaty, we pulled the canoes onto a grassy beach at Liverpool. With Eli on his leash, we headed to the corner store for a good chilling milkshake. This small-town namesake

Susquehanna below Sunbury

of Liverpool, England, held an interest greater than its size. In the slow pace of a summer afternoon, porches were full of oldtimers sitting, staying out of indoor heat and outdoor work. Not everyone was as lucky, though; one man spent the day tearing the roof off an old, weathered barn. The cashier at the grocery store talked of a Harrisburger who wanted to come north to Liverpool, "to get away from it." The Good Samaritan Hotel remains from long ago, when canal passengers would spend the night on their way to Sunbury or Williamsport. Curiously, Liverpool is a one-sided town; the west side of the main street is full of houses, the east side nearly vacant. The canal filled the space on the river, or eastern side, and now Highways 11 and 15 carry a different kind of traffic over the same route. Mahantango Mountain stands in rugged prominence across the wide and rocky Susquehanna from the town, and downstream is the steeple of a Millersburg church. I hesitated only a moment or so to take a picture of the Liverpool Bank, but during that time an off-duty clerk stopped his car to find out "just what my business was, anyway." Small town protectiveness soon changed to friendliness as we talked about the river.

Swinging our canoes to Millersburg across wide, shallow flats, we found the real riverfront town. With no road or railroad interrupting its view to the water, the hamlet had an integrity and oneness with the Susquehanna. The riverfront park at the Fish Commission's access area was a community center. A gang of shouting children ran on the wet, slick surface of a log and leaped into the current. They seemed to care nothing about an eddy

Millersburg Ferry

Bob Banks, Susquehanna River below Millersburg

of yellow foam and blackened refuse behind their plankway. Neither sudsed-up water nor the raucous play of the kids disturbed the flock of ducks, which swam just beyond the splashing divers. Townspeople came to the riverfront to walk or to sit and watch, while river people like us wandered up the street to buy another late-afternoon refreshment. Across the waters the sternwheel ferryboat pushed its way toward us, water rising at its wake to catch the flash of 6:00 P.M. sunlight. As the ferry drew closer, watchers on shore took closer looks, shaded their eyes with cupped hands, and smiled at the pilot's adeptness as he swung the ferry to dock. Jack Dillman owns and runs the fleet of two boats, one being an old "coal digger" and the other a new custom-built model. Only four sternwheel ferryboats remain in the country. Dillman's career as a riverman began when he was eight.

"The current you can see, but wind is the worst since you can't tell what it'll do. Northeast always makes for trouble. If we get blown on the rocks, usually I can get it off myself, but sometimes four or five of us get out there up to our waists to pry her off." But groundings are scarce, and Jack has never had serious trouble.

Having to move on and make camp before dark, we paddled toward the shadow of Berry Mountain. An evening sun cast its golden light over the river, and as swirls and eddies gleamed with the sun's warmth, the sound of whitewater grew in a slow crescendo. "The best water of the trip is just ahead," Bob said, and we swung the canoes to the right, narrowly missing a

Photo by John Lazenby

Rockville Railroad Bridge, Susquehanna River above Harrisburg

submerged rock. I took the camera and began shooting pictures of the action that was all around us. Unlike most Susquehanna riffles, this one didn't quickly end but continued plunging on and on.

We spent the night on an island and left in fog early Tuesday. From Clarks Ferry Bridge and the mouth of the Juniata, there was just enough whitewater to keep us alert. Above the massive Rockville railroad bridge, the whole world suddenly began to froth around us. With a few excited strokes we saved ourselves, but we had nearly lost control in one of the sudden and steeply dropping outcrops that cross the river. The story of a Renovo native came to mind. In 1917 the river adventurer canoed from home to Harrisburg, then capsized in rocky waters. Having lost most of his gear, he ended up catching the next train going upriver.

Shielded from Harrisburg by the trees of McCormick Island, we drifted silently within twenty-five feet of a dozen Canada geese. Our lunch stop was on the western side of an island—"Poison Ivy Paradise," we called it. You couldn't step out of the boat without stepping in the itchy stuff. Like Squatter's Island in Williamsport, those city-owned islands were vacant of campers, children fishing, one-day runaways, and rowboat adventurers. They must be around, but where?

The dam in Harrisburg sinks a boater every now and then, its drop being nearly invisible from waters above. Not paying attention, we soon were within a paddle's throw of the spillway. Making a sharp turn, we headed for the eastern shore, where the spillway is reduced to an incline. At lower

Harrisburg, from the Susquehanna River

levels it could be negotiated, but now it promised a bath in stinking water. Tying ropes to bow and stern, we carefully walked the canoes through the chute, avoiding the labor of another unloading and reloading operation. At the lower end of the capital city, sewage and other wastes drove us to the western shore and into cleaner waters.

A sultry and humid haze added little to the next twelve miles of paddling—a reach that was the least scenic of the trip and in fact the only stretch of continued ugliness in the whole river. Lower Harrisburg, Steelton, and Olmstead Airport covered the eastern shore with industry, earthen fill, and junked wreckage. We passed the Three Mile Island nuclear power plant, which was still under construction. In many ways, that was a turning point of the voyage. There would be good water ahead, and we'd even see another osprey, but the squalor of the river that afternoon was a bitter illness from which we would never really recover. There were no more Sterling Runs for drinking water, no more Loyalsocks for chilling swims, no more picturesque Mahantango Mountains, no more Liverpools or Millersburg Ferries, and not even very many more islands creating remote back channels. Mostly there would be power plants with monolithic profiles, transmission lines sweeping toward distant homes and factories, and dams impounding the river into flatwater of half-day cruises.

Hill Island, just below Middletown, is distinguished as the only hill island in the river, reaching 230 feet above the water's edge. We shot the rapids around the west side and entered the headwaters of York Haven Dam.

Photo by John Lazenby

Three-Mile Island nuclear plant (1977), Susquehanna River at Goldsboro

The impoundment is built at the site of Conewago Falls (not to be confused with Conowingo), which used to be a series of steep rapids, dropping
twenty-three feet in three-fourths of a mile. For nearly two miles the
breastwork of the structure extends *up and down* the Susquehanna while
crossing it. We docked at the hydroelectric power plant, and meeting a
maintenance crew, I asked, "Where's the best place to carry canoes
around?"

The Metropolitan Edison employee cocked his hard hat, thought, and
then pointed. "Go across the walkway, down the tracks, past the power
plant. Get onto a service road, and then down below, you'll see the river."
We started thinking of two loads each for gear, wishing we'd made the trip
seventy-three years ago when we could have shot Conewago Falls and
taken our chances on a cold spill. "Wait a minute," he said. "A while back,
some canoes came through, and we picked them up with a crane and carried them around the dam. Go see the superintendent, and he'll tell you
what we can do."

Twenty minutes later, we paddled up to a loading dock, fastened straps
around the boats, and watched Don Leakway and his friendly crew swing
our canoes out of the water and onto a flatbed truck. We unloaded below
the dam and set out again for the Chesapeake. It turned out that law required the utility to portage canoes—the dam blocks the river, so they carry
us around. All the other power companies did the same thing.

It was noon when we pulled our canoes onto the beach at Columbia. A

Penn Central crew took advantage of the setting, having lunch and a few hands of poker. One tall railroader intercepted me as I went back to the canoe for my maps, and we ended up telling the men of our trip. "Everybody used to canoe on the river," one said, "but more people have motorboats now."

Hard on our backs was a northwesterly wind as we drifted into Lake Clarke—the impoundment of Safe Harbor Dam. The river broadened to an immense width and spaciousness. Sailboats darted with the wind, then tacked and cut a ragged groove in choppy waters. The dam was soon ahead, while an ominous and blackening sky caught up from the rear. Amid a mountain of accumulated driftwood, tin cans, and dead fish, we tried to beach the canoes, having to haul them over the trash for lack of any other landing area. Cold raindrops the size of green peas came with thunderclaps and flashes. Derelict cranes and an endless array of scrap metal surrounded us, offering the perfect lightning target. The place was no "safe harbor" to us, so we were interested in getting out of there, quick. We'd just started the long walk to the power plant office to ask for our portage, when a uniformed guard drove up. One thing led to another, and we ended up under a shelter along Conestoga Creek for the night. The plant supervisor wanted us off the river and away from the plant for safety and so offered special permission for us to spend the night in the company's park nearby.

Settling into a quiet nighttime rain, the storm passed, and a brilliant morning welcomed us for our last day on the Susquehanna. By 11:00 A.M. we beached at Holtwood Dam. Water flows over the top of Holtwood, making it a hazard to river travelers in the past. Billboards now warn approaching boaters, and a shield has been constructed to keep unsuspecting tourists from getting too close. A few years ago, a couple on their first date raced two other speedboats to the dam, and not watching the water ahead, they sailed over the sixty-foot wall of concrete. Miraculously landing rightside up, they reached for nearby life jackets and swam away without an injury. The boat sank, but the couple later got married. As the local media put it, "They're going to take another chance."

The afternoon was a wild one. Our course through expansive Conowingo Dam included the stiffest paddling, highest winds, and most turbulent waters of the journey. Two, three, and then four-foot high waves rolled beneath us, our boats pitching, surfing, and bobbing like corks. Luckily the wind was still behind us, otherwise we would have been forced in. Not wanting to be far from an emergency landing, we clung to the western shore. A stiffness and exhaustion moved up my back and into my shoulder as we pushed around the exposed and windiest point of land where Peach Bottom nuclear plant is built on rock and earthen fill. We found a rhythm for surfing; power strokes would send the canoes skimming down the breaking crest of a wave for an exhilarating instant, then back into the trough we'd go.

Holtwood Dam, the lower Susquehanna

Relief came with Glenn Cove, the marina where we landed and tele-
phoned for portage around Conowingo Dam. A utility truck came in an
hour or so, hauling us to a relaunching area. Conowingo is on the "fall
line," or that point where tides and upstream travel end. In 1608 John
Smith sailed to Conowingo Falls, but no further.

In an early evening stillness, we entered the final phase of our journey.
The Susquehanna current took its last plunge downward; low rapids would
swirl for only another mile. Seagulls and sailboats thrived on a flatter arm
of the Atlantic Ocean ahead. Two hundred and forty-five miles of river
had brought us to elevation zero. In much the same way that we had
loaded and embarked at Karthaus, Lock Haven, and Williamsport, we cast
off the Maryland shore, only now for the last time, to see the end of central Pennsylvania water. Two railroad bridges and the monumental highway crossings of Interstate 95 and U.S. Route 40 stole that last final breath
of peacefulness that might have gone with the broadening of river into bay.
Instead they accented the difference, making it possible for an old river-

front local to respond to a question by saying, "Yep, right there, the last bridge, that's where the Susquehanna River ends and the Chesapeake Bay begins."

We could see the end below and the bay with its different world of water beyond the river's flow. Salt water mixes with fresh, forming a different ecosystem and a way of life unlike any we had seen on the Susquehanna. Yachts and beaches, tides and endless waters—none of it is like the river, but none of it would be there without the river.

And so, with a certain completeness to our paddle stroke, with the fullness of nine days of sun and eight nights of listening to water as it passed our camp site in a continuous drop, and with visions of the Pennsylvania heartland forever in mind, we finished our cruise on that quiet evening.

The variety of scenes and the differences between them drove us to get on the river and ride it to the sea. A chilling taste of Sterling Run in the West Branch Canyon, the rapids at Millersburg, a sultry afternoon's heat at Steelton, and the orange-blanketed sky at the Chesapeake vitalized our lives again. Seeing the river world around us gave a sense of discovery that many of us enjoyed only when we were younger.

We know the river best when we see it firsthand. Draining the waters of our lands, the river gives us, and all the places we know, a timeless continuity. In the past it brought logs, rafts, canal boats, and settlers. It brought shad runs, before dams blocked the migrating fish's journey to spawning beds. It brought floods, in 1889, 1936, 1946, and 1972. Today it brings over three million people a year to its edge for recreation.

The next time we make the trip, will we still have the wild West Branch Canyon? Will bass and walleye be thriving at Williamsport, or will an acid slug poison the river as before? On those long stretches of water where you see nothing but islands and mountains—how many more power plants, bridges, and industries will we see instead? Change is unavoidable, but changes on the Susquehanna may show a different kind of progress. The next time we go down to the Chesapeake, or the next time you do, a wilderness might remain—not through neglect but because people want to keep it that way. You might see a trout darting above Lock Haven, and the orange stain of mining might have faded from the rocks. Bald Eagle Creek might run without the suffocating load of silt that we saw. Instead of a tangled web of power lines, maybe a lighter hand will have put new lines where they won't be seen. Maybe the trailers will be above the flood plain, leaving low shores for high waters.

At our fifth camp site, we had looked at the dark brown river and thought of an early canoeist quenching his thirst with Susquehanna water. That day was long ago, and it won't come again in our lifetime, but we just might be able to swim without wading through foam, like the children in Millersburg. Yes, we'll look forward to going another time, and maybe a wilder, more scenic, less polluted Susquehanna will carry us to the sea. But for you, go now, because you might never see it this good again.

Protection for the Waters of Pine Creek

More than any other stream of northern Pennsylvania, Pine Creek has received the attention it deserves. Too much, some people would say. "With all those reports and studies you could paper the creek from Galeton to the Susquehanna River," a resident of the area remarked at a public meeting in 1976. Some fruitless efforts have been undertaken along with other necessary and productive ones—enough that the case of "Tiadaghton"* has been a valuable experiment in what works and what doesn't.

October 2, 1968
Most of the talk at the time dealt with Hubert Humphrey and Richard Nixon. One or the other would soon be elected President. News articles included nothing about rivers: "Hanoi Aides Reject Humphrey's Plan"; "House Ethics Panel Will Study Votes Cast for Absent Members"; "Gallup Poll Finds Many Traditionally Democratic Voting Groups Are Switching to Nixon"; "Vassar Going Coed; Plans Williams Link." In an action that attracted no headlines, Lyndon Baines Johnson signed the National Wild and Scenic Rivers Act into law. The absence of theatrics and excitement was understandable. Five years earlier, in 1963, a study of the Interior and Agriculture departments included the seeds of a National Rivers System. Groups like the Wilderness Society pushed the program, and Representative John Saylor of Johnstown, Pennsylvania, sponsored legislation. Most people agreed that the idea was a good one. It had the support of conservation interests, yet it didn't raise strenuous objections from groups involved in dams or river development, since the law posed few major threats to foreseeable water resource projects. The secretaries of Interior and Agriculture recommended the bill, saying, "We have enjoyed wild rivers as have our forebears for generations. Our descendants deserve the same opportunity." The Act states:

> It is hereby declared to be the policy of the United States that certain selected rivers of the Nation which, with their immediate environments, possess outstandingly remarkable scenic, recreational, geologic, fish and wildlife, historic, cultural, or other similar values, shall be preserved in free-flowing condition, and that they and their immediate environments shall be protected for the benefit and enjoyment of present and future generations. The Congress declares that the established national policy of dam and other construction at appropriate sections of the rivers of the United States needs to be complemented by a policy that would preserve other selected rivers or sections thereof

---

*An Indian word meaning "river of pines." There is a controversy over the location of the true Tiadaghton. Some evidence suggests that the Indians' Tiadaghton was Lycoming Creek and that white men moved the name further west to "stretch" the treaty agreement.

Pine Creek below the village of Blackwell

in their free-flowing condition to protect the water quality of such rivers and to fulfill other vital national conservation purposes.

The force of the Act was apparent:

The Federal Power Commission shall not license the construction of any dam, water conduit, reservoir powerhouse, transmission line, or other project works . . . on any river . . . which is hereafter designated for inclusion in that system, and no department or agency of the United States shall assist by loan, grant, license, or otherwise the construction of any water resources project that would have a direct and adverse effect on the values for which the river was established.

In other words, no dams.

Eight rivers were granted such protection on October 2, 1968, and twenty-seven others were identified as possible National Rivers, their status to be determined by Congress or the Secretary of Interior after study was completed. Pine Creek was one of those twenty-seven, along with the Clarion, lower Allegheny, upper Delaware, and Youghiogheny of Pennsylvania. The upper West Branch of the Susquehanna narrowly missed inclusion.

Four years later, the national study began. Since the end of the logging era in 1909, the creek had been a popular fishing stream, and over the years millions of tourists viewed the "Grand Canyon of Pennsylvania" from overlooks near Wellsboro. Now Pine Creek was considered nationally significant, and this distinction gave rise to interests and actions of importance.

August 18, 1969

On those hot summer days the flies hover and swarm, and it's hard to keep them out of your eyes. In a routine he had followed for thirty-five years, the forestry professor cleaned his pipe and lit it again, cherry-scented smoke driving the worst pesky bugs away. This was at least the hundredth time that he untied an old wooden canoe from his car roof and carried it to the edge of Pine Creek. He patiently loaded the craft with gear, and in the slow, deliberate manner that takes hold after one's fiftieth season, he pushed the red canoe away from Sugar Island, leaving his car near the site where John English and his family built the first homestead in the valley two hundred years before.

Many times Fletcher had sensed a difference in Pine Creek, but as everything changes to people who live long enough and look hard enough, he didn't give it much thought. Today was different. A blanket of algae completely covered the creek bottom, unlike anything the forester had seen in the fifty-four years that he had visited the family camp site. "The water's low and the temperature's high. But this comes from more than natural causes." He continued to reason while he paddled. When the canoe scraped the stone beach at Fletcher Camp, his idea had formed.

"A total water study is needed," he decided, "one that can identify the cause of overfertilization in Pine Creek, one that would reach to the headwaters." The upstream towns of Wellsboro and Galeton were scarcely regarded as part of the same creek—they were so different from the valley, and the seventeen-mile-long canyon separated them. "It should be done," he concluded, "before our problem becomes too big to solve." He always liked the idea of using research to *do* something.

It wasn't long until Fletcher's students were scouting, wading, sampling, testing, and recording at a score of stations along the creek. Coliform pollution counts were plotted and graphed, and when preliminary results were in, the professor was ready to talk. He left a troubled group at the Wellsboro Rotary Club with charts that showed pollution from their community exceptionally high, depressing the life of the stream for miles. His data alarmed conservationists and fishermen, precipitating formation of a Pine Creek Watershed Association, whose first task was to gain improved treatment by upstream towns.

The brilliant algae bloom of August was the result of voluminous quantities of silt that had washed downstream from a highway construction project fifty miles away. As is often the case, the initial impetus for the water-quality research turned out to be one of the less significant findings. Little did Dr. Peter W. Fletcher know that a water-quality study would go so far. The concern that it raised, coupled with inclusion of Pine Creek in the National Wild and Scenic Rivers Act, served to spawn efforts on a diversity of fronts and to involve growing numbers of people. Fletcher promoted this idea: "When Pine Creek is evaluated for Scenic River designation, we should make sure that it qualifies." Unanticipated by the professor but arising from his study, many actions followed: a crack-down on industrial pollution, new orders for Wellsboro and Galeton to upgrade their treatment of waste, inspection of on-site sewage facilities, public acquisition of prime open-space lands, designation of state Wild and Natural Areas, and a host of other projects aimed at a quality environment along Pine Creek. Problems were not to be neglected.

February 23, 1972

"I'd like to call this meeting to order." In a small, overheated conference room in Williamsport, sixty-seven people were crowded elbow-to-elbow. "I'd like to thank you all for coming; it's good to see so many people who are interested in Pine Creek." Walter Lyon, director of the Pennsylvania Bureau of Water Quality Management, began the meeting on a note of cooperation that would become characteristic. The Pine Creek Task Force worked through effective leadership.

It also worked because of the people who attended. As soon as the chairman introduced himself, everybody else did likewise. An incredible array of interests were represented. One room held township officials, industrialists, strip-mine interests, municipal sewer authority directors, environmentalists, county planners, university professors, and the whole spectrum of state agencies—the many bureaus of the Department of Environmental Resources (DER), the Department of Transportation, Fish Commission, Game Commission, and others. They all came in response to an invitation by the Secretary of DER, Dr. Maurice Goddard.

The formation of the Task Force was a climax of protection activities up to that date. Dr. Goddard had been flooded by requests and complaints, the variety and complexity of which, he decided, warranted a special organization to be headed by one of the Department's chief administrators. "Finally we can sit down face to face and discuss the problems of Pine Creek," responded Trout Unlimited representative Bob McCullough, a man who initiated many protection programs, devoting years of effort to this stream and others. "A lot of these state agencies don't know what the others are doing, let alone the different counties," he added. When criticized that the new group was just another forum for discussion, McCullough responded, "Talking isn't necessarily *bad*. Things are going to happen, you wait and see. Nobody likes to have an accusing finger pointed at them in meetings like this. If the Department agrees to do something, they'll be reluctant to return to the next meeting without having it done."

It was apparent from the February 21 session that something had changed, that a new thrust to correct pollution and other problems along Pine Creek had indeed begun. Early objectives were stated: to adopt water quality standards, to seek national designation, to establish good land-use management programs, and others. The chairman established six committees and appointed a chairman for each; these became the working groups reporting back to the Task Force at quarterly meetings. No one knew, however, of the diversity and depth that would mark their involvement in the Task Force. Highway design standards, rural solid waste collection, dam construction, flood-plain zoning, and myriad other issues would be pursued.

April 18, 1972

"You, sir—do you know which end of a paddle to put in the water?" The middle-aged balding office administrator to whom the question was directed looked around. His eyes were two big question marks.

"Why, sure I do."

"Good. Then you will go in my canoe." That is how outfitter, Pine Creek native, canyon expert, and ace raconteur Ed McCarthy selects his partner. "When you drive a car you steer from the front, and that's where you put your best tires, but remember, a six-man Avon raft is not a car. You steer from the back, and that's where your big stick should be. Show them, George." George, the district forester, pushed his raft this way then that, with a rudderlike sweep of his paddle. "Any man who does like George will come back alive, I promise you."

Then the suntanned riverman turned to a representative of the National Park Service. "Sir, your rainpants will stay dry if you leave them rolled up, but if you wear them, *you* will stay dry." He leaned toward the park representative. "In the canyon it will be as cold as the shady side of a banker's heart. Wear 'em!"

While ten people boarded rafts and six climbed into canoes, Ed McCarthy extolled the virtues of the day. "Never will you see such a morning as this, gentlemen. The three greatest variables on the face of the earth are water, weather, and people, and we've done exceptionally well on all counts today."

We began, not with a rush but into a sluggish current, paddling the final half mile of Marsh Creek to its confluence with Pine. This was the long-awaited beginning of the National Wild and Scenic River Study. Many actors were present for the drama. The federal Bureau of Outdoor Recreation (BOR) headed the team and would be in charge of preparing the study report. The National Park Service and Forest Service were represented but made sure that their agencies didn't end up having anything to do with Pine Creek, since none of the land is federally owned. Exceeding the expectations of the Fish and Wildlife Service expert, a bald eagle soared northward up the creek, no more than fifty feet over our heads. The Army Corps of Engineers sent a biologist rather than an engineer. Two park planners from the state selected a covered or decked canoe rather than a raft, and paid for the increased maneuverability with leg cramps caused by crowded seat compartments. Representatives for county planning agencies were there, along with those of the Susquehanna River Basin Commission and The Pennsylvania State University.

We beached at Owassee, where the creek takes a tortuous bend to the

The Owassee Rapids, Pine Creek Canyon

east and water thunders through a narrow, rock-studded chute. "How did the canyon get here, anyway?" one of the federal officials asked.

"The glacier stopped at Ansonia," I began to explain, "where we started the trip. A moraine of sand and stone blocked the southern channel until lakewater covered the lands up above—"

"Then it all broke loose at once?" he interrupted.

"And carved the canyon when it did," I finished.

"That makes the geology outstanding enough," the official concluded, referring to the special qualities that a river should have if it's to be eligible for the National Rivers System.

Pine Creek was still carving the canyon as we floated on its high waters through the treacherous bend at Owassee, over rapids at Bear Run, and past high cliffs called Falling Springs, where cold water seeped from the mountain and splashed in a series of exhilarating cascades that ended in the swollen creek.

Later that afternoon the group met in the upstairs bunkroom of "Mallard," one of Ed's rental cabins.

"What do you think the classification ought to be?" the group leader asked.

"One thing's for sure—it can't be wild." With this statement nearly everyone agreed, since they knew the railroad paralleled the stream.

"The railroad's there, but it doesn't provide access to the creek," another person countered, "and this is about as wild as any large streams get in the northeast."

Canoes at the Owassee Rapids

"The shorelines can't have any development if it's to be classified as wild," answered Noll Granzo, the study leader. "Besides that, it can always be *managed* as a wild river, even if it's classified as recreational or scenic."

"Somewhere along the way things became more crowded. I don't know if the whole area could be scenic," the Forest Service representative said.

"One mile above Slate Run there are a lot more cabins," a local authority answered, "and then at Cammal—"

"Cammal!" interrupted a BOR official. "Cammal's where the power line is, isn't it? We must have looked at that butcher job for two miles!"

"But just below it is one of the best stretches of the whole creek," a younger man added. "The west shore from the power line to Jersey Mills is wild—no road or railroad. A lot of people stopped there at Solomon Run

Pine Creek Canyon near Bear Run

to drink water, and all of the public lands on that side are being designated a Natural Area by the state."

"Well, if it's going to be 'scenic' to Jersey Mills, shouldn't we just call the whole thing scenic?" a state man asked.

"That would have the most local support," the other answered. "Less likelihood of encouraging recreational development." And so "scenic" it was.

Later that spring, the Bureau of Outdoor Recreation conducted public meetings at Wellsboro and Jersey Shore. The study was delayed several times, and additional public meetings were held in 1975. The issue had

Pine Creek Canyon near Pine Island Run

Rafting through the Pine Creek Canyon

become exceedingly complex by that time, with passage of a State Scenic Rivers Act and with other activities of the Pennsylvania Department of Environmental Resources. The sessions became mired in questions regarding DER land acquisition and whether or not parcels at Tiadaghton village would be condemned. BOR officials announced that Pine Creek would qualify as a National Scenic River and that it should be administered by the state, meaning that the federal government would not be involved in acquisition, recreation development, regulation, or management.

Some months later, the Army Corps of Engineers selected Cammal as one of the six sites in the Susquehanna Basin for a hydroelectric dam analysis, thereby raising fears that hadn't existed before and support for national designation. The state Department of Environmental Resources opposed the dam and also opposed National Scenic River designation for reasons that were to become heatedly controversial.

February 2, 1973

Two Lycoming County planners walked into the cinder-block fire hall. You could hear the tension. The truck was parked outside to make room for thirty cold metal folding chairs, and a new furnace blew warmed-over air in too-small quantities, so that everybody left their dark winter coats on. "That's him, right there," a woman said, as the two men entered. While their arrival quieted some people, it caused as many others to say something to their neighbors.

"Quite a turnout here, fellas," one of the township supervisors said to the pair of guests. He smiled, but he knew this wasn't going to be pleasant. "How'd ya want to handle it?"

A few minutes later the meeting began. "These two fellas agreed to come up here today to talk about something that could affect all of us on Pine Creek," the chairman began. "Flood insurance."

"Zonin', you mean!" echoed a voice from the back. That was the extent of the introductions.

The planners attempted an explanation, but it didn't last long. "The idea is that the federal government will help pay the cost to insure development that already exists on the flood plain, but only if the township takes steps to see that flood damages won't get worse."

"It's zoning, isn't it?"

"The township would zone the flood plain in order to discourage construction of buildings that would be damaged during floods."

"Three years ago they were talking about zonin' up here, and I don't see that this is any different. We ran it out then and we'll run it out now." There was a chorus of agreement from the crowd, by this time obscured in a haze of cigar, cigarette, and pipe smoke. A few older Pine Creekers stood in the back and listened, their minds not made up. From the middle of the crowd, a whiskered man put up his hand and began talking at the same time.

Marsh Creek, a major Pine Creek tributary

"We had zoning in Williamsport and you couldn't even trim your trees."

"Sir, I don't know what you couldn't do in Williamsport, but for zoning to meet flood-insurance requirements, you don't need to be concerned about tree-trimming," the county man answered. The old Williamsporter looked at the flannel-shirted man next to him, and between chews on his tobacco, he said, "Won't even be able to prune those apple trees of yours."

Taking a subtler approach, a man in the front asked, "Taxes'll go up, won't they?"

"Taxes might go up, but not because of zoning," was the answer.

"Just wondered. Where I came from they had zoning, and then taxes went up." He went on to say that increased taxes resulted when public sewer lines were added to his old Bucks County neighborhood. The planner tried to explain that with the right kind of zoning in a rural area like Pine Creek, the people could make sure they'd never need sewer lines, but the Bucks County man's firsthand experience of tax increases had impressed the others.

"You say that state law requires us to zone everything in the township?" This man was one of the few who lived in the mountains, away from the valley. Everyone knew what was coming.

"The law says that if you zone, all of the township needs to be identified under one land-use classification or another, in order for all landowners to get equal treatment," came the answer, though in some ways it didn't make good sense.

"In other words, we have to live with regulations so that a few people can get insurance paid for." Since it was not a question, the officials didn't answer. "I say we've been takin' care of ourselves for years and we can keep on doin' so."

That did get a response. The other county planner mentioned that 1972 flood victims received $1.5 billion in relief, and that the federal government spends $1 billion per year for flood-control projects. "There are a lot of people here who collected taxpayers' money to recover from the flood."

The discussion went on for some time. Stubbornly, and with foresight, the township supervisors refused to take immediate action to reject the program but left it alive. "We've got to think about this," they said, and adjourned the meeting.

The flood insurance program began with the prospect of a better future: new flood-plain development would cease, while the program would recognize and help people who had already invested in property. But the implementation has been ragged with compromise, indecision, cost, and delay. Initial mapping prepared by consultants for the Federal Flood Insurance Administration, a division of the Department of Housing and Urban Development, was regularly, grossly inaccurate. Flood-plain restrictions and standards for compliance were set at a level that may not afford true protection to the homeowner or to the riverfront. New construction in the "flood fringe" zone is permitted if it is raised on earthen fill, but this displaces water and aggravates the neighbor's problems. No zoning whatever is required until FIA finishes their mapping, which can go on for years in some municipalities. Places like Lewis Township on Lycoming Creek belligerently rejected zoning, yet enjoy the benefits of flood insurance that is 48 percent subsidized by the general taxpayer. "Floodproofing" requirements increase the cost of construction, but can still result in widespread flood-plain development, where economic loss and disaster remain inevitable.

For all those shortcomings, the program still has merit, for it offers the incentive to zone—maybe enough incentive to convince people who wouldn't do it otherwise. It could be one of the most important measures of river protection all over the country, resulting in less flood damage, more open riverbanks, less water pollution, and more scenic streams. Both the state and federal wild and scenic river programs encourage zoning, but neither can require it. In Pennsylvania, the authority to zone lies solely with the township or county.

Despite the objections at the grim meeting on Pine Creek, a few weeks later the township passed a resolution agreeing with the flood insurance program. Those residents who wanted it had apparently convinced many of the others that it was a good thing. Other townships did likewise. For all the damage it created, the flood of 1972 left a clear impression on people's minds and, with some, a willingness to go about life a little differently in

Pine Creek above Cedar Run

Rowing across Pine Creek at Waterville

the future. Incentives were strengthened, as municipalities were required to participate in order for federally insured mortgages to be available. Some people now look at local land-use regulation as a way of protecting what they have, and the idea of restrictions on development of flood plains and steep slopes has some support. In 1972 only one township along the creek had zoning, but by 1975 nearly all of them were in the process of adopting regulations. If they are adequately administered, these local land-use management programs will represent a very large step toward protection of Pine Creek.

May 1975

The Pine Creek Valley Preservation Association was organized in early 1975. It represented an advance in the approach toward protecting the creek. For the first time an organization of valley residents and landowners existed, whose responsibility it was to speak for local people. Residents had always been involved in the Watershed Association (which became inactive in 1972), in the Task Force, and as individuals, but now there was a group of residents. While the basic objective of the Association is to "keep Pine Creek the way it is today," the motivation to organize came largely from a single event and the fear it brought that land would be condemned.

For a number of years, a program of land acquisition by the Pennsylvania Department of Environmental Resources had been going very well. That is, many local owners wanted to sell their land for open-space protection, the state had money to pay fair if not top prices, and everybody was pleased with the arrangements. A prime 500-acre tract with 1½ miles of creek frontage was one of the first to be bought; the Nature Conservancy acquired it and then resold it to the state. Its owner had been the most outspoken critic of government, and so it was said, "If they pleased Stu, they can probably please anybody." All in all, a few thousand acres of open space were added to the state forest through purchase of valley lands. Nearly half of the stream corridor is now in public ownership, which is one reason so much of the region has been protected.

The state then turned its attention to the canyon. Where Campbell Run had carved a notch and created a delta, a small village had grown in the logging days and was given the name Tiadaghton. For eight miles above and eight below, there are only a half-dozen cabins. A foully pitched mud and mountainstone road drops from the rim, providing access of a sort, and over the years, loggers' homes became hunting cabins or were left to rot. Partly due to a threat of commercial campground construction, partly due to the canyon's designation as a National Natural Landmark and a state Natural Area, and partly because Tiadaghton is the only developed area of the seventeen-mile-long reach, the Department of Environmental Resources decided that it should acquire the private parcels. To establish public ownership of the canyon seemed to be a worthwhile objective. Unfortunately, officials decided to send a letter to each owner rather than initiate the more personalized contact that had proven so successful to date. The letter included implications of condemnation:

> The purpose of this letter is to inform you that the Department proposes to acquire your property, leading to the consolidation in public ownership of the topographic feature known as the Pennsylvania Grand Canyon. . . . Upon acquisition of your property, the Department, as a condition of settlement, will permit you to continue your occupancy of the improvement on the property under the terms of a lease-back arrangement for a period of five (5) years.

This letter caused a reaction much akin to the spontaneous combustion of an overloaded hay barn.

"They want our land so people floatin' down the creek won't see any houses. What's it hurt to see a house?" one of the owners questioned at a public meeting held by the federal Bureau of Outdoor Recreation in the wake of the Tiadaghton letter.

"First they buy Tiadaghton, then Blackwell, Cedar Run, Slate Run, and right down the creek they'll go," said another. This was never the intent of the state, but since its intent had never clearly been presented, it was left to speculation.

The Preservation Association was formed. Its first major task was to determine DER's position on the buying of land. State officials said that no condemnation was contemplated at this time, an open-ended statement that heated the issue like bellows on a blacksmith's fire. The Secretary of the Department personally met with several residents, saying that no land would be condemned below the canyon. "That's fine, as far as his word goes," a resident said, then added, "I believe him, but how long's he going to be the Secretary?"

A written position was forthcoming as a Department policy statement which said, "The Department will continue to acquire land on a willing-seller, willing-buyer basis, hoping particularly to acquire those lands adjacent to the stream that are as yet undeveloped but which have high development potential."

The Preservation Association soon became more than a single-issue group. Amid the confusion of other events, a consortium of private utility companies proposed a statewide concept of energy "parks," where ten to twenty power plants would be grouped on one site. Ten preferred locations in Pennsylvania were selected, and one was at the edge of the Pine Creek watershed. Dams at Cammal, in the middle of the scenic river study reach, and at Keating, on the Susquehanna's West Branch, were listed as "most suitable" sites for water supply, raising adamant objections of the new group. Shortly thereafter, the Army Corps of Engineers identified Cammal with six other sites in the Susquehanna River Basin for hydroelectric studies.

A major and complex question now came before the group. The Scenic River Study by the federal Bureau of Outdoor Recreation recommended designation of Pine Creek in the National Wild and Scenic Rivers System, if

The village of Slate Run

the Governor requested inclusion. The Department of Environmental Resources would recommend the stream for designation in a State Scenic Rivers System. What will be the best for Pine Creek?

March 15, 1976
It was no surprise when the Pennsylvania Department of Environmental Resources released a statement in March of 1976, expressing opposition to the designation of Pine Creek in the National Wild and Scenic Rivers System. Some people were aware of Department's concerns since passage of the federal act in 1968, when state officials remained disinterested or downright unhappy with the idea of national rivers in Commonwealth territory. The Department stated:

> For several reasons, the Department does not recommend the designation of Pine Creek as a component of the National Wild and Scenic Rivers System. National designation would: 1) result in increased publicity, 2) attract more people to an area that is already on the brink of overuse, 3) would not provide federal funds for acquisition or development beyond those that are already

Local campers at Tiadaghton

available to the Commonwealth under other grant programs, 4) national designation would remove the flexibility and control from local government and state land management agencies by adding an extra level of administrative control, and 5) would give decision-making power to a federal agency that is far removed from the day to day contact that now exists between local residents, local government, and state land management agencies.

Questions and counterpositions came from many quarters.

"Don't trust 'em," a resident said. "Look at Tocks Island Dam—Pennsylvania supported it even though the other three states didn't."

"Wouldn't the federal government be a 'court of last resort' if we have problems?" another asked.

"They might think they can stop a dam," a local attorney said, "but there are other states that can't."

County planners tried to document the issue of increased publicity, which could lead to increased use. It was apparent that rivers belonging to state or federal systems see an increase in use, but then so do streams that are not so designated. The Youghiogheny soared from 5,000 floaters per year in 1968 to 100,000 in 1977, and the reach in question is not in any system whatsoever. The Allagash of Maine, which was the first river to be federally designated, though administered and managed by the state, has seen a general climb in recreation volume; however, inclusion in the national system seems to have caused little change in the rate of increase. Most important, opponents of the publicity-overuse argument pointed out that Pine Creek can normally be canoed in the springtime only—water level is too low through summer months. If federal status were to attract more people, they would likely be coming from distant areas mostly during summer vacations rather than in other seasons. Since the creek can't be floated from June through September, summer canoeists are not likely to come. People who live close enough to canoe on spring weekends will know about the stream whether or not it's nationally recognized. The experience of Little Beaver Creek of Ohio supports this reasoning—no increase has been noticed by state officials. The creek is in the federal system, but water levels are generally too low for summer floating.

Other questions center around the wisdom of involving a federal bureaucracy. "It's a valid concern," a BOR official pointed out. "But we should look at the record of the Bureau—Ohio and Maine officials are administering national rivers, and they are well pleased with federal involvement. The federal government does not exercise any administrative control. All we do is approve of a state-prepared management plan certifying that the stream will be adequately protected."

"Once the stream is designated," says Dick Mosley, who directs Ohio's river program, "you don't know the federal government is there."

A local person, who was concerned about the Army Corps' dam proposal, argued in favor of national designation: "More government means more red tape and more difficulties in doing certain things—especially in building government dams!" But it seems that the state has too often been entangled in federal requirements and paperwork. Problems with other programs have led to fears that a river designation may be more trouble than it's worth.

The opinions of local residents vary. Distrust for the state is prevalent. "The day could come when the state won't have the power to stop a federal dam," as one landowner said.

Bill Painter, who directed the American Rivers Conservation Council, summarized the situation: "Federal involvement provides legal protection against a federal project; state designation gives political protection at the state level only," meaning that the governor would likely disapprove of a dam.

"The New Melones Dam on the Stanislaus River of California was an example," said Brendt Blackwelder of the Environmental Policy Center in Washington. "The state Water Resources Control Board attempted to restrict the activities of the federal Bureau of Reclamation, but the court ruled against them. Fortunately, the decision was partially overturned. North Carolina could not stop a dam on the New River—federal designation was required. The long-term prospects are that pressures for dams will be great. Since all of the good sites for Army Corps projects have been exhausted, the criteria may become less restrictive in the future, allowing dams where they are not considered economically or politically feasible today."

With its national river recommendation, the Bureau of Outdoor Recreation also encouraged inclusion of the creek in the state scenic rivers system, but Pennsylvania, as we shall see, has problems of its own.

August 23, 1978
Early in 1978, the Department of Environmental Resources held hearings on the
subject of state scenic river designation. Officials met a hostile audience in Tioga
County, and a few weeks later the local senator blasted the program. DER Secretary
Goddard had his fill of the controversy and called a halt to the study.

It was another public meeting, with Peter Fletcher calling people together at the Whitneyville Fairgrounds, east of Wellsboro. The intent was
to determine local sentiment about the state scenic-river study, and special
guests included the two state assemblymen, Warren Spencer of Tioga
County and Joe Grieco of Lycoming County.

Spencer denounced the scenic-river program. "The sewage treatment
that DER wants us to do in Wellsboro would make our waste purer than
rainwater," he said. His statement, besides being exaggerated, had no bearing on the river designation.

"I'm against it because of the tax base we'll lose in Tioga County,"
Spencer continued. But examination shows only 190 acres of private land
in the Tiadaghton area, the only place where substantial acquisition may
occur in Tioga County. Total tax income from these parcels would be
under $200, with less than $30 going to the township. Road maintenance
to serve the Tiadaghton owners costs the township $500 to $1,000 per
year.

Joe Grieco described how he grew up near Pine Creek, saying that these
were his people, and they were not going to be ignored or abused by DER
again. He didn't elaborate on the scenic-river program; it paled into unap-
proachable irrelevancy beside the question of liking or disliking government.

The Lycoming County Planning Commission was called upon to explain
its position: "We favor federal and state designation for two reasons: it's
the most certain way to prevent a dam from being built, and the valley
needs priority attention from the state to manage the recreation problems
that we have. DER should cope with solid waste, access area maintenance,
and other issues, and scenic-river status is the only way it'll get done."

Most of the evening was spent in a collective grumble about the tax base
and the problems of trash and township road maintenance.

The Preservation Association president spoke with uncommon clarity and
reason. "We want a better management plan—one that tells us what's going
to happen and how the problems will be solved. We want to know that
DER will have the money they need to do the job. Then we'll decide if we
want the program or not."

One township supervisor drew applause with a proposal to liquidate the
state land. Two other municipal representatives stated their disapproval of
the scenic-river program, since their townships are located above the section of creek to be designated. This added to the confusion: those who
were in the proposal wanted out, and those who were out wanted in.

Agreement was almost unanimous—"people problems" were affecting the
creek and the lands along it. Recreation creates problems that indeed need

solving, but this was seen as a reason *not* to designate Pine Creek. It was a stunning victory for ambiguity and irrelevancy. The president of the Pennsylvania Federation of Sportsmen's Clubs reported on his group's position: no more land should be bought in Pennsylvania by the federal government. However, this subject had never been proposed or considered for the Pine Creek area.

After such enlightenment, a vote was taken in democratic fashion. Results were conclusive. People at the meeting did not want Pine Creek in the state scenic-rivers system.

It may be an endless controversy, Pennsylvania's Pine Creek. If a stream as fine as this cannot be effectively dealt with and protected, can any? Can we learn from these mistakes, can we satisfy the conflicting demands? This is a simple case. Consider a complex one, where the dam-building forces are organized, where the state doesn't own half the riverfront, where urbanization is rampant, where coal reserves are ready for stripping, where the water is already polluted.

In some ways Pine Creek offers little reason to hope that we can look at the long-term future and make decisions to preserve a river. Yet the hope remains that we will do it. Many conservation efforts have struggled along without support until a major threat is upon the scene. Unfortunately, support is often too late. In the process of aimless waiting for things to get so bad that everyone recognizes a need to act, will the desirable qualities of the place be whittled away to a skeleton?

There is no such thing as no plan. When knowledge of alternatives exists, inaction is as deliberate as action, leading effectively to unwanted ends. Will elected officials be interested in the facts of the case and in everybody's future? The state is more than a device for serving immediate desires; it exists to serve the needs of all, including future generations. That's why the state has responsibilities that we as individuals, or politicians as individuals, aren't accustomed to. Many people hold the state accountable for the immediate future. Who holds it accountable for the distant future?

Maybe a new management plan will gain the support of local people and then local representatives. Maybe statewide support for protection of Pine Creek will override local opposition. Or maybe things will slide toward tomorrow, where we'll find Cammal Dam awaiting, a power plant at Cherry Flats, or a bustling Pocono resort at Cedar Run.

Troutwater, Canoewater: The Loyalsock

Loyalsock enthusiasts may well be the most avid of all river supporters in northern Pennsylvania. Few problems diminish the creek's appeal, and the smallness of the stream seems to elicit strong feelings. Many people feel that a big river can take care of itself, so to speak, and that a little more pollution won't hurt, but a narrower and cleaner stream like the "Sock" leads to more responsible conclusions. Residents, fishermen, canoeists, hikers, and campers are all interested. The Loyalsock has many excellent features:

Trout fishing is outstanding, especially in the lower creek below Forksville.

Whitewater canoeing in the springtime is hard to equal anywhere. The upper reaches are for experts only, and national slalom races have been held at Worlds End State Park.

The Loyalsock Trail is one of the finest and most popular hiking trails in Pennsylvania.

Worlds End State Park includes camping and picnicking areas with wild creek frontage and scenic views.

It all begins in a swamp above the little town of Lopez, where some waters drain to Mehoopany Creek and others fall to the west. The watery volume gradually increases, and with the addition of Lopez Creek, a larger Loyalsock is formed. At very high levels, a kayak journey can begin here and run to the West Branch of the Susquehanna River. The canoeable gradient is greater than any other waterway in Pennsylvania. After Lopez, the stream plunges and winds in Class II rapids for seven miles, over half of which has wild shorelines with no roads or buildings. Natural acidity from upland bogs is greatly augmented by drainage from coal mines, depressing the biology but not the scenery of the upper creek. Pollution eventually becomes diluted in the downstream descent.

At Route 220 the truly spectacular Loyalsock begins, with wildwater plunging over ledges again and again. Gravel and glacial boulders are brilliantly white, unlike the grey and brown riverstones found on other creeks. The Loyalsock Trail begins here, following a course through hemlocks and hardwoods to Dutchman's Falls on a tributary stream. A highlight of the Loyalsock is reached two miles east from the trailhead, where waters thunder over the Haystacks—a collection of large rounded rock outcrops that are scattered from one side of the creek to the other, creating an impassable barrier to all but the most expert paddler in any but the highest of water. The Haystacks are a popular camping area, and deep green pools above and below the rapids attract summertime swimmers. This four-mile stretch of the creek has no roads or railroads, and for a full eleven miles

Loyalsock Creek above Worlds End Park

between Route 220 and Route 87, the rapids are consistently rated a difficult Class III, for accomplished, experienced paddlers only. The gorge is
wild and scenic, with foaming whitewater, glistening rock gardens of riverstone, high cliffs at water's edge, and the blackened shade of matured
forests. This section and lower reaches have been recommended as high-
priority candidates for the Pennsylvania Scenic Rivers System.

Worlds End Park includes campgrounds, picnic areas, a creek to explore,
and views from high rocks above the Loyalsock. Whitewater races annually
draw large crowds and competitors from all over the East. The "old-time"
park appearance has survived at Worlds End, with log cabins, log headquarters, log guardrails, and logs everywhere.

Three more miles of heavy whitewater leads to the village of Forksville,
most noted for its 126-year-old covered bridge. Below the old logging
town, the mountains rise higher, but rapids are subdued to Class I and
II—excellent for the experienced paddler in an open canoe. Scenery is still
superb, though the valley is wider and more open, with a flood plain that is
often farmed. Riverbank cabins and trailers gradually increase along the
way.

Fishing on the lower Loyalsock is excellent, with a native population of
brown trout, brook trout, and other species. Shaded banks, cold tributaries,
and deep holes keep the water temperatures low. While most large streams
warm to eighty degrees and more in the heat of August, this one usually
doesn't, and its trout prosper. Along with other popular fisheries of Kettle

Creek and the Sinnemahoning's First Fork in the north central highlands, the "Sock" is big enough for excitement and variety, yet it is small enough to wade across in the summertime.

Conflicts arise between trout fishermen and canoers. Problems between the two groups have become serious on some rivers. The most notable of these is the Au Sable in Michigan, where thousands of anglers come to the cool, spring-fed waters, meeting thousands of canoeists who are attracted by the beauty and ease with which the small river can be traveled. The two factions should be compatible, one would think, since both have an appreciation for the same resource. Usually this is the case, except that boaters splash and make noise, scaring away fish. There lies the problem. In Pennsylvania the situation is seldom serious, since trout streams are usually too low to float in summertime, and since there aren't a lot of canoes in most places. Unfortunately, there is friction at times.

We were paddling through midmorning sunshine below Forksville, where a long pool stretched ahead of us and ended in a ragged-edged turbulence of Loyalsock rapids. A brown trout, motionless against the gentle current, sensed our coming and darted for cover.

"Here comes another lousy canoe." An irritable voice carried across the quiet waters from the head of the riffle. Muffled and garbled in the current below, another man said something I couldn't hear. "I said, here comes another blasted canoe!" he repeated, a little louder this time, taking his cigar out of his mouth and holding it in his left hand with his line. The trout fisherman didn't intend me to hear his remark, as evidenced by his big grin and "Fine morning, isn't it?" as we passed quickly by. We, of course, agreed, maintaining whatever social lubricant we could in a curiously strained relationship between freshwater enthusiasts.

His grievance irritated me at first. "He must think he owns the stream," Cindy said. We saw no other craft all morning, and there had been few canoes on the creek since May, when water drops to rocky levels. Knowing that neither he nor I was the worse for either of us being there, I shrugged it off. We wouldn't disturb his water—he wasn't even fishing but walking up the riffle, though that isn't always the case.

Fishermen have been knocked down by rafters who are unable to control their craft, and floaters have been stoned by shoreside anglers who aren't able to control their tempers. Ignorance is often the reason for lost trout and high blood pressure. Floaters call out, "How's the fishing?" as they paddle past, and the man in hip boots answers, "Fine, until *you* came along." I was once the guilty leader of a group who swarmed down on a peaceful angler—in front of him, behind him, and still coming from above. Having been too far ahead of the group to avoid the confrontation, I then gathered the small fleet of rafts and canoes together at the first gravel bar and gave them a few easy rules to follow:

Canoeing the Loyalsock above Worlds End Park

Never run into a fisherman.

Always pass a fisherman in single file, taking the same route as the boat ahead of you.

When the fisherman is wading deep enough, go behind him, where he's not casting.

If you can't go behind him, stay as far away as you can get.

Move as quietly as you can and quit paddling if the current will carry you.

Be friendly but don't overdo it—a lot of fishermen really don't like your being there, and there's no sense chatting when they only want you to leave.

   Timing of stream-oriented recreation is critical to avoid confrontations. If floaters begin traveling no earlier than 9:00 A.M. and get off the water by 5:00 P.M., a lot of problems will be solved. The angler who is serious about his fun will be hunting trout while paddlers are breaking camp or making camp. Generally speaking, midday hours are preferable to boaters anyway, though there are exceptions. In early evening stillness and then in long shadows and the golden light of sunset, I've enjoyed paddling and fishing a six-mile reach of stream below our house. Rarely would I see another fisherman on those trips, as it was usually a weeknight instead of a weekend.

Special regulations may be necessary where boater-angler disputes are severe, or where recreational use damages the riverine environment, the life-style of local residents, or the scenic river experience itself. On some waterways, permits are now required for visitors to float the stream, with various restrictions on party size, camping sites, and use of motors. In most cases these streams are in the national or a state scenic-rivers system, and much of the shoreline is publicly owned. In order to enforce permit or river-use requirements, it is necessary that boating access points be limited in number, thus enabling a public agency to economically administer regulations from a few selected locations. Neither scenic designation, public ownership, nor limited access is the case on the Loyalsock, and so conflicts between boaters, fishermen, and other people have to be resolved voluntarily and through an understanding of one another. A little courtesy on the part of all groups can avoid confrontations and hard feelings—differences that are minor when compared to concerns for clean water, wildness, and free-flowing streams.

Water quality is clearly an issue to the fishermen and canoeists, and both groups have worked together to protect the Loyalsock. A strip mine was proposed that would discharge water into Scar and possibly Ketchum runs, both flowing into the "Sock" between the villages of Forksville and Hillsgrove. Stripping, the mining advocates say, will "clean up" a problem that was left from abandoned coal-mining operations. Many people disagree. "There's no problem that needs cleaning," says Ron Thompson, biologist and president of the Loyalsock Watershed Association. "We've tested the water to prove it, but you don't need a sampling bottle and white laboratory coat to see trout in those streams."

After a mining permit was requested of the Department of Environmental Resources in 1975, conservation groups barraged them with protests, and the Department agreed to make no decisions until a public hearing was held. This case could be significant as a guide for future actions elsewhere, for two primary arguments against the mine have great relevance to other Pennsylvania streams:

Opponents argue that surface rights to the land are of significant public value and should take precedence over mineral rights. While the land belongs to the Commonwealth as state forest, the minerals are controlled by a mining company.

The streams emanating from the mining area are of high quality, supporting native brook trout and feeding a clean Loyalsock. "Water quality of Scar and Ketchum runs is excellent but fragile," Thompson says. "Sandstone and natural acidity allow little buffering capacity, so any acid dis-

Ketchum Run, a wild tributary to the Loyalsock

charge is likely to have a devastating effect." Since these streams are clean, mine opponents say we should take special care to *keep* them clean, restricting coal extraction to watersheds that are already acid-polluted, of which there are an ample number in Pennsylvania.

Loyalsock below the village of Barbours

Below Scar and Ketchum runs, the Loyalsock passes the villages of Hillsgrove, Barbours, Loyalsockville, and Farragut. A potential dam site has been identified by the Army Corps of Engineers near Barbours, though it is not being studied or recommended. Scenery, exciting rapids, and clear water continue to the Susquehanna. While 34 percent of the watershed is in public ownership, much of the lower valley is not. Access is possible at Moore's Country Store in Barbours, the mouth of Wallis Run, the Game Commission Farm at Loyalsockville, and at the Susquehanna's West Branch, where the borough of Montoursville has built a park.

Here the Loyalsock has a unique distinction, for it is the last large and unpolluted tributary to the Susquehanna. All of those below this point are muddied and clouded in comparison. Across Pennsylvania, this stream is one of the cleanest, but also one of the most fragile. Thus the effect of even minor degradation becomes important. The question is not how much pollution is added but how much quality is lost. With several groups working to protect the Loyalsock, maybe it will remain undamaged and keep its special appeal.

Moshannon and the Canyon:
A Dam Could Change It All

High in coal country near Philipsburg, Moshannon Creek curves through peaceful forests of low wetlands, then drops and rolls into whitewater before meeting the West Branch of the Susquehanna. It is sometimes said that this mountain stream has a split personality—much of the watershed is ravaged by mining, but the corridor and gorge of the winding creek remain a splendid wild path. While upper portions of the 274-square-mile drainage area offer little in scenic or recreational assets, the lower twelve miles are of rare value, as rapids push through a narrow valley that has only one bridge crossing and no paralleling roads or railroad.

We were lucky. The day we cruised, it was ninety degrees, and water roared after three inches of rain had soaked the northern highlands. More often, the necessary high water comes when snow still clings to northern slopes and ice persists in glazing rocky bluffs above the stream's edge. From the village of Winburne, we enjoyed peaceful paddling through slow water. Vegetation crowded the shorelines, like the sand rivers of northern Wisconsin or Minnesota. Hemlocks, rhododendrons, birches, and other plants hung over the banks, enclosing the traveler in a capsule of green. Now and then the water's edge was punctuated by a hugh white pine, its two-foot-diameter trunk grossly out of scale in a region where forests have been repeatedly cut. Passing through flats that looked like wetlands of the north, we could understand the Moshannon's name, which is translated as "Moose Stream" from an Indian dialect. This was probably one of the few Pennsylvania ranges that moose inhabited prior to the arrival of white people in America.

Near the towering twin bridges of Interstate 80, whitewater began. It grew and multiplied from there on, each rapids seeming to breed two more. When we reached the Route 53 crossing at the mouth of torrential Black Moshannon, we had dumped water from our canoe twice, and then the fun really began. Half a mile below the bridge, we stopped on a gravel bar to scout for an ominous-sounding rapids ahead, then ran the channel to a cautious right, staying paddle-length distance from a massive boulder that capsized a small rubber raft in front of us. When the wider Susquehanna was almost in sight, the last descending pitch of the "Mo" swept over rocks buried deep in rough current, creating a roller-coaster of buoyant highs, then thunderous falls. Half a dozen children were there with inner tubes, so we beached at the end of the rough water, where Cindy swapped a few cookies for a rubber tube and went splashing off into the rapids, this journey being a much wetter one than her first.

Even though the water level is often too low for traveling, the Moshannon has become a popular whitewater stream and a favorite for enthusiasts

Moshannon Creek near the West Branch Susquehanna

Moshannon below Interstate 80

from nearby Pennsylvania State University. There is, however, one major problem—acid mine drainage. Since low water levels show a brightly stained streambed, many people refer to the Moshannon as the "Red Mo." The orange precipitate is usually called "yellow-boy." It results from iron content in the overburden of shale that is removed when stripping bituminous coal. As long as shale stays buried, its acid, iron, zinc, and other vile components remain inert, but when it is hauled to the surface by dragline, bulldozer, or dynamite, air and water mix to form a toxic head of poison. The Moshannon is one of the most polluted streams in coal country, though it is far from unique—there are 1,350 miles of acid-bearing water in the Susquehanna basin alone. Fish cannot tolerate the acid waters, and this ironically is one reason that the wild Moshannon shorelines have survived. Without fishermen and pressure for seasonal homes, the inaccessible reaches of the waterway have remained without roads or cabins.

There is a unique advantage to designating these streams as recreational rivers: canoeing and camping can be enjoyed without the fisherman-versus-boater conflicts that are becoming more common elsewhere. By encouraging canoeing on the Moshannon, the upper West Branch, Sinnemahoning's Bennett Branch, and the Clarion, boating pressure on prime fisheries can be reduced. This presents one of the few opportunities to segregate stream uses without the necessity of regulations.

After the excitement of Moshannon whitewater, the Susquehanna's West Branch seemed slow and easy, though we enjoyed the more relaxed pace to the village of Karthaus. There the twenty-four-mile canyon began, with its steep-sloped, forested mountains rising high to the plateau above. This section of the Susquehanna is always the most enjoyable, as the road is left behind at Karthaus. Except for the railroad and a few coal tipples that are used to load trains, the traveler has the river to himself. After camping along a tributary stream that was pure and unaffected by mine drainage, we spent an easy day paddling and drifting toward the village of Keating.

In 1977 the Scenic Rivers Task Force for Pennsylvania identified the upper West Branch as the number one priority for State Scenic River Study. Moshannon, Black Moshannon, and nearby Mosquito Creek were also highly ranked. Keating Dam would flood large portions of them all. With a proposed location near the mouth of Sinnemahoning Creek above the village of Keating, the dam would be about 400 feet high and its reservoir nearly 50 miles in length. The 1976 cost estimate was $700 million—one of the costliest water projects in the country's history.

Starting in 1934, the Army Corps of Engineers identified several possible West Branch impoundment sites. Through four different studies, the dam-building agency has reviewed the idea, and in 1972 they reported a lowly 0.5 benefit-cost ratio, meaning the dam's cost equals twice its value. The Corps indicated that there was no likelihood of the project proceeding. In

June of that year, the worst flood on record blanketed the lowlands of the Susquehanna basin, and damage was widespread—$1.5 billion in federal and $290 million in state money were spent in relief. With renewed interest in a federal project, yet another analysis of Keating was begun. Strong support was voiced by the West Branch Valley Flood Control Association, a group that opposed construction of a dike around the disaster-prone city of Lock Haven. On June 28, 1976, at Lock Haven, the Army announced a new benefit-cost ratio for the dam of 0.8, additional benefits largely being an increased value of hydroelectric power.

Reaction to the new figures was rapid and madly divergent. Flood-control interests resented the attitude of Army personnel, who implied that the project would not reach the one-to-one benefit-cost ratio that is required for consideration by Congress. River protectionists raised many concerns:

Mine drainage will form an acid lake, requiring specialized hydroelectric equipment, mine reclamation, or water treatment, the costs of which were not considered.

Recreational benefits for the reservoir were being calculated, but no accounting was made of the significant natural-river recreation activity that would be lost when the rivers are dammed.

In 1972, 260,000 kilowatts of power were projected. In 1976, with a *smaller* dam proposed, 500,000 kilowatts were projected.

The value of electric power has increased, but so have costs of heavy construction. Has this adequately been evaluated?

A local official did some estimating and reported that the annual interest on $700 million would pay for the combined budgets of eleven central Pennsylvania counties, and a fee of much less than $700 million would buy flood insurance for all flood-prone property in the same region for 100 years—the estimated life of the dam. Advocates of nonstructural solutions asked, "Why not buy downstream riverfront lands that occasionally flood instead of permanently flooding upstream lands that *never* flood?" The dam's cost would be enough to acquire much of the flood plain area. Some downstream communities were in favor of the project for reasons of flood control, with upstream areas opposing the dam because it was their land that was to be flooded. Another concern related to an energy "park" proposal, advanced in 1975 by a group of Pennsylvania utility companies. Clusters of ten to twenty power plants would be located together. Pine Glen, almost adjacent to the potential reservoir, was one of ten candidate sites in the state, and Keating Dam was referenced as a "most suitable" location for water supply. "You don't ever have to worry about an impoundment *that* expensive being built," a federal official stated. Yet the Pennsylvania Department of Environmental Resources requested that the Army continue to study and evaluate possible additional benefits of water supply through low-flow augmentation to the Susquehanna River.

The West Branch Susquehanna Canyon, below Moshannon Creek

Other programs of the state run counter to the impoundment: with DER's recommendation, the Environmental Quality Board designated a wild area on state forest land at Burns Run, just above the dam site. The Fish Commission was intending to acquire boating access areas along the threatened section of the river. Pennsylvania's recreation plan identifies this reach of the West Branch and Moshannon as part of the "North Central High Mountain Area," where natural aspects of the land would be conserved for all time. The document recommends "the perpetual protection of these areas from further invasion by highways, private leases, utility rights-of-way and other forms of commercial development which remove inherent public benefits in the name of progress."

In the midst of the controversy, the House Appropriations Committee held hearings on a proposal to dike the city of Lock Haven. Dam proponents testified that a "greater" solution was needed. The Northcentral Highlands Association and the Canoe Division of Penn State Outing Club advocated nonstructural protection, recognizing the false sense of security that dams and dikes create, as illustrated by Rapid City, South Dakota, and Wilkes-Barre, Pennsylvania, in 1972. With the illusion of protection, more development occurs on the flood plain, adding to the damage potential from an exceptional storm. For Lock Haven, environmental groups supported the dike as offering faster, more complete protection with manifestly less environmental impact than the dam, at $1/23$ the cost. About half of the flood-control benefits of Keating would be due to flood reduction in Lock Haven—figures that were developed assuming there would be no dike.

The issue drags on, an indication of questions to come on other Pennsylvania rivers. The St. Petersburg Dam proposal on the Clarion was also revived after the Hurricane Agnes flood in 1972. Cammal, in the heart of the recommended National Scenic River reach of Pine Creek, was chosen by the Army Corps as one of six sites in the Susquehanna Basin for hydroelectric analysis. Sinnemahoning was another. Possible dam sites are scattered like buckshot. The upper Delaware alone has six "potential" locations as well as familiar Tocks Island. Importantly, motives for dams are likely to change. Flood-control objectives that were popular in the past have been under consistent and effective criticism, and a national consensus toward flood-plain management has developed—a "Unified National Program for Flood Plain Management," as the United States Water Resources Council calls it, stressing nonstructural alternatives toward reduction of flood losses. Section 17 of the Water Resources Development Act of 1968 authorizes funding of nonstructural alternatives such as relocation of development from the flood plain, but the Office of Management and Budget has refused to approve the programs.

Recreation benefits have likewise been under fire. With more and more impoundments for motorboating and fewer rivers to run, the evidence is clear that we need both, and wild rivers are now a scarce item. New attention is being given to hydroelectric power in a national effort to decrease dependence on foreign fuel, but the most suitable sites have long ago been developed. Furthermore, problems of coal-generated electricity have theoretical and often feasible solutions; hydroelectric dams eliminate the river permanently, for all practical purposes, and there is no theoretical or feasible way to replace the natural river.

Water supply may become critical in the future, and this may become the most important reason to build dams. With growing populations in regions where water supplies are inadequate and where nuclear power plants consume vast amounts of cooling water, something will have to be done in order to meet or to change projected future needs. The traditional water-resource and engineering approach is to build more dams in order to make more water available. Conservation of water is scarcely discussed, just as conservation of fuel was only lately given even token attention. Questions of equity will be debated as never before: should the qualities of headwater regions be sacrificed for distant urban centers? Who will make the choices, and who will gain the profit, and will those who pay the costs—financially and otherwise—be the ones who also receive the benefits? How will our social consciousness cope with trade-offs between short-term needs for electricity and the permanent loss of irreplaceable resources?

To the natural river advocates, the issues of economics or population displacement may be important, but the main issue remains the natural qualities of the stream itself—the value and the need for wild places, the beauty and the meaning that can come from a part of the earth where rivers flow free. This is an interest not quantified in the system that calculates benefits and costs. Such numbers fail to represent many real values. And for those benefits and costs that *are* calculated, the numbers can be arbitrary, easily manipulated to suit the biases of the manipulator.

It may become axiomatic that to maintain a free-flowing natural river, it must be designated as such in a national or state scenic-rivers system. If not, the waterway is "available" for other use. How do we decide which rivers should run free? Obviously, if we are to meet society's needs as now

The West Branch Susquehanna Canyon near Moshannon Creek

perceived, all streams cannot be preserved. Which have the "outstanding" qualities referred to in river protection legislation? Some questions will be answered by professionals in water-resource, scenic-river, and other fields, as evidenced by the growing effectiveness of guidelines such as the Principles and Standards of the United States Water Resources Council. But many of the answers will only come through people and the political process—all of us.

We camped for a night near the dam site at Yost Run, a churning brook trout tributary to the West Branch. This was the deepest and most exciting part of the canyon, where wooded mountainsides climbed 1,000 feet above. The river rolled on and on in moonlight, shimmering with a dark reflection of silver as I looked up toward the distant Moshannon. I thought of the Susquehanna's near-miss: this section of river was in the original National Wild and Scenic Rivers Act of 1968, but because of the local representative's opposition, the West Branch was deleted before the bill passed. Maybe there will be another chance.

Opposite: Juniata River below Huntingdon

Juniata and the Life in a River

The Juniata is a slow-moving river of central and southern Pennsylvania that is praised by people who fish for smallmouth bass, muskellunge, suckers, carp, and sunfish. It is a large watershed, 3,404 square miles, ranking in size only behind the big six of Pennsylvania: the Ohio, Allegheny, Monongahela, West Branch of the Susquehanna, Susquehanna, and Delaware. Waters parallel and then slice through the high, sandstone-covered mountains of the Ridge and Valley Province.

The landscape along parts of the Juniata and its tributaries reflects what many people feel to be a classic Pennsylvania image—a well-blended scene of farms and forests, mountains and streams, all together in a way that makes you feel good again, like you've seen a part of the older Penn's Woods and not a land that gets remodeled every twenty years. Spruce Creek is that way where farms roll across a limestone valley. Steep-sided Tussey Mountain forms the background, and fertile trout waters wind southeastward. It's a peaceful scene for folks who live at Pennsylvania Furnace, Graysville, or Seven Stars, for springtime fishermen, for children who like to swim in summer and cross-country ski in winter.

Three main branches form the Juniata: Raystown, Frankstown, and the Little Juniata. Raystown begins in the mountains near Bedford. A recently completed Army Corps of Engineers' dam floods the lower valley, an area that now attracts motorboaters as well as fishermen. Frankstown starts above Hollidaysburg, and the Little Juniata begins near Altoona, flowing northeast to Tyrone. It cuts through a scenic gorge below Spruce Creek village and then meets the Frankstown above Huntingdon. This is where the Juniata River begins, and where I began a slow-moving, six-day canoe trip to the Susquehanna.

Nearly every community has its back to the river, and Huntingdon is no exception. A vacant lot along the waterfront showed some promise of an urban park, bearing a sign that gave credit to a redevelopment authority and the United States Department of Housing and Urban Development for clearing away an area damaged by recent floods. Clearance wasn't quite complete, so amid bricks and broken glass, we set the canoe into a foam-filled eddy and loaded our gear. Eli, our black labrador retriever, looked at the water but passed on his normal pretrip ritual of swimming and jumped straight into the boat. Away we went.

While the scenic Juniata offers many interesting features, one needs to be either fishing or lazy for full appreciation. You can focus your eyes out there on nothing and let your mind recuperate. I spent a good while reading from a comfortable propped seat in the bottom of the boat, disturbed more often by Eli's sighting of a turtle than by dangerous rapids.

Clear waters now come from Raystown Branch, as most of the silt from farmland and streambank erosion has been deposited in the reservoir. While the lower reach of Raystown is almost sterile and seems to be less productive from a fisheries standpoint, the clean water helped to dilute the cloudiness and gray-colored riverbed that we saw in Huntingdon.

A pole is an excellent piece of equipment for the Juniata: often the river is shallow with a sandy or stony bottom, allowing the boater to stand in the stern and push his craft toward the Chesapeake. It's easier than paddling or rowing. Just above the Route 829 bridge, I poled through a luxuriant bloom of algae and aquatic plants; watery green leaves and yellow flowers covered the river in thick masses full of insects and riverine creatures.

Fishing access areas are plentifully provided by the Pennsylvania Fish Commission, and camp sites are easy to find. Usually an island or vacant shoreline is available where you won't bother anybody and nobody will bother you, which is a high-ranking objective of an easygoing canoe trip. One night we camped on rocks below the town of Newton-Hamilton, where waters boil over ledges and through chutes. It's the only major rapids of the river and a scenic highlight, with the houses and church of the village reflected in a long upstream pool, and a fury of whitewater and high ridges enclosing the downstream view. Killdeer, great blue herons, green herons, kingfishers, and sandpipers feed everywhere on the gluttonous supply of food that the Juniata provides.

At small towns like Mt. Union you can stop for groceries or ice cream on a hot day. We climbed craggy sandstone ridges above Route 22 for a view of the river and the community of Mapleton. Lewistown is the only urban center, followed by a long reach of flatwater where it's safest to paddle the shoreline, away from powerboats and waterskiers. While the river from Huntingdon to Lewistown is winding and often remote from the highway, the lower reach becomes wider, straighter, and in some sections crowded by four lanes of Route 322.

The real highlight of the Juniata is not the life *of* the river so much as the life *in* it. Many Pennsylvania streams are wilder, cleaner, faster, and more scenic, but no others of this size have the incredible array and amounts of waterborne creatures. A wealth of mussels, crustaceans, and fish are obvious to the traveler or angler. Smaller animals and aquatic plants are less noticeable but more essential to the Juniata ecosystem. Life changes with varying conditions: riffles, pools, sunshine, shade, shallow water, deep water, winter, summer—all lead to distinctive communities.

The food chain, as ecologists call it, begins with very simple organisms. Algae are vital ingredients, forming a slippery slime on rocks, a green carpet at the riverbed, or a swaying wave of filaments in the current. With leaves and other drifting plant debris, the basic building blocks of river life are formed. Bacteria and fungi break plant matter down, while insects and mussels are filter feeders, sifting particles and nutrients. These are primary

Juniata rapids, town of Newton-Hamilton in background

consumers, feeding on detritus or food matter of the current. The mayfly and caddisfly are two important insects that convert plant material to animal tissue.

Pale yellow wings of the mayfly are often imitated by the trout fisherman's artificial lures such as the Quill Gordon, American March Brown, Hendrickson, and Green Drake. These represent the adult phase, when thousands of the mothlike insects will rise from a watery surface. Fishermen say that a "hatch is on." Caddisfly larvae are well adapted to riffles of the Juniata and other streams, as they glue sand particles together in a protective home that may be tubular, conical, or rectangular-shaped. Pebbles will even be added to weight the larvae and assume a stable and stationary home in fast water.

Juniata below Mapleton

Secondary consumers are middlemen that eat small creatures and in turn are eaten by larger ones. On the Juniata, these include the dragonfly, damselfly, hellgramites, and some minnows. The dragonfly can be seen darting over the river on a hot summer day, though this represents only a short-lived adult stage of its life. As a nymph, the dragonfly lives in mud, on wet stems of plants, or even under rocks. Its lower lip, or labium, injects prey that includes insects, crayfish, tadpoles, small fish, and fellow nymphs. Through the year, a skin might be shed a dozen times until finally an adult emerges. Soon its long double wings stiffen for a new life of wildly acrobatic flying. No other insect has the excellent vision afforded by the dragonfly's protruding, compound eyes, used to hunt mosquitoes, the mainstay of its diet, and leading to the nickname "mosquito hawk." These and the closely related damselflies mate while airborne, and afterward they often fly in tandem. The male, now expendable as far as the species is concerned, flies above, protecting the egg-bearing female from attacks of birds. Females can sometimes be seen with only a portion of a male abdomen attached, the remainder having served as a meal to a fast-diving swallow.

Crayfish in large numbers crawl along the Juniata shore. At some places they can be found under almost every rock. These are also middlemen, scavenging leaves, dead insects, and sometimes live insects, then being eaten by fish, mink, raccoons, and birds. Favorite Juniata dinner sites of the raccoon are littered with hundreds of crayfish remains. Rocks become covered with dismembered claws.

Trout are plentiful in many tributaries and headwater reaches, but the river itself far exceeds their maximum tolerable temperature of seventy-seven to eighty degrees. Bass, on the other hand, do their best in temperatures of seventy-nine to eighty-three degrees, and they find ideal conditions here. Muskellunge are also popular game fish due to stocking programs, and some catches reach over forty inches in length. Many Juniata fish are bottom dwellers, characterized by flat bellies, underslung mouths, strong pectoral fins for propping, eyes near the top of their heads, and small swim bladders since they don't have to float to the surface. Suckers and catfish, for example, are adapted to scavenging and cleaning the riverbed. Many fish have a progressive diet as they grow larger, first feeding on algae and detritus, then insects, invertebrates, small fish, and larger fish. One challenge for the fisherman is to match bait or lures to this widely variable diet—to offer fish what, in fact, they want to eat.

Reptiles and amphibians can also be seen on the Juniata. Salamanders live in dark, damp places under stones, laying eggs in the water. Turtles often crawl onto logs that overhang the river, spending much of their time in the water but laying eggs on land.

With the abundance of aquatic life, many water-loving birds make their homes along the brushy, forested, or eroded shorelines. Sandpipers pick small insects and crustaceans from gravel or sandy edges. Kingfishers rattle their call, diving for minnows, frogs, and crayfish and living in a hole near

A young fisherman's catch, Juniata below Lewistown

swallow nests along a steep bank. Green herons and the less common yellow-crowned night herons fish the shallow waters, but showiest of all the Juniata birds are the great blue heron and the egret. An adult great blue is four feet high with a wingspan of six feet, eating small fish, frogs, salamanders, crayfish, and snakes. On land, they'll catch mice, often dunking them in the river for a Juniata dip before swallowing. Mergansers are diving ducks with sleek bodies, strong wings, and webbed feet for chasing small fish. I once removed a fishhook from a tangled merganser, and even though his wing feathers were broken from thrashing, he disappeared in an instant, swimming so far under water that I never saw him come up. To most people, mergansers are foul-tasting and inedible, and that is likely the reason so many can be seen on Pennsylvania rivers.

Along with larger fish and birds, the muskrat, mink, and raccoon are at the top of the Juniata's food chain. Plants and mussels are food for the muskrat. It, in turn, is favorite prey of the mink, a small, shy, beautiful fur bearer. Raccoons are true omnivores, eating almost anything: frogs, salamanders, crayfish, mussels, fish, nuts, leaves, turtles' eggs, birds' eggs, nest-lings, corn, picnics, fishermen's fish, and garbage. Their hand-shaped tracks can be seen on sandy beaches everywhere along this and other Penn-sylvania rivers.

We, of course, are also at the top of the Juniata food chain, feeding on smallmouth, musky, sunfish, and suckers, rather than algae, mayflies, and crayfish. While higher members of the chain benefit from the food pro-cessing of primary and secondary consumers, they also stand to suffer most from imbalances and toxic chemicals. Concentrations of many pollutants tend to accumulate as they rise through the food chain. While a mayfly may absorb small amounts of a hazardous substance, the minnow that eats 100 mayflies may consume 100 times that amount, the bass that eats 100 minnows receives 10,000 times that amount, and the fisherman who eats 100 bass may be dining on 1,000,000 times the pollution dosage. Since we know that toxic wastes like mercury, lead, and Kepone have been dumped into fresh water, it leads one to wonder just how safe Juniata fish are. Many people remember when you couldn't travel through the town of Ty-rone without choking on the sulfur-filled air. What about the water? What is it doing to all these fish we're eating?

Bill Parsons, an engineer, and Jerry Miller, a biologist for the Pennsylva-nia Department of Environmental Resources, had some of the answers. "Pollution used to be severe at Tyrone, but it's greatly reduced now," Par-sons said, "and the paper mill at Williamsburg closed, so we've seen pretty substantial improvement in water quality. Old paper mills used toxics like mercury, but we don't have trouble with it now. The big problem is at Roaring Spring, on a tributary to Frankstown Branch. Appleton Papers, a division of National Cash Register, is dumping copper, phenol, aluminum, color, odor, heat, and other pollutants." He paused. "Ever drink a dark brew with a nice thick head on it? Well, that's what the creek looks like. It's similar to the problem that we used to have at Tyrone, only worse. It's the worst pollution in central Pennsylvania, but Appleton is paying fines and trying to clean it up. Platinum-cobalt units of color went from 2,500 to 750 in four years, but the water standards limit is fifty, and it's supposed to be met by 1983. It's hard to see how the problem can ever be eliminated, with such a big operation on such a small stream." In 1979 agreements were reached whereby Appleton will more effectively treat their waste and will move their discharge to a larger stream.

"Sewage has been a problem in the past, but a lot of that's improving," Parsons went on. "Bedford just started their advanced treatment plant, which should do a real good job on the upper reaches of Raystown. Franks-town Branch has a tough start in Hollidaysburg and Altoona, but advanced treatment is only awaiting federal funds. Then there are local problems at Huntingdon and Lewistown, but no great impact. Near Lewistown, Honey Creek was *named* for its sewage problem, but half of that is being treated now, and the other half should be in a few years. Mining up Raystown Branch has just about sterilized Six Mile Run."

"It's hard to tell what paper mills or other industry did to fish in the past," Miller explained, "except that we know the river is extremely productive in spite of it. The Juniata's chemistry is excellent for growing things—the limestone origin of many tributaries helps, with high quantities of dissolved calcium and magnesium. There must be a new hatch of mayflies every two weeks during summer months. Crayfish are everywhere, and we found at least fifty rock bass under one boulder when we were electro-shocking during a biological survey."

While smallmouth draw fishermen and a muskellunge population is building, the Juniata could also become a key in the reintroduction of shad—a prized but nearly forgotten game fish. Susquehanna shad runs are legendary. A few old-timers recall thousands of them migrating from the Chesapeake Bay to spawn throughout the river basin. High dams blocked the shad's only route to survival. Conowingo in Maryland, and York Haven, Safe Harbor, and Holtwood Dams in Pennsylvania didn't include fish ladders, which in other rivers allow anadromous, or seagoing, species to complete their spawning run. Efforts have been made to capture and truck the fish around high Conowingo Dam, but without much success. The Pennsylvania Fish Commission is now rearing shad on the Juniata, hoping that the

Poling a canoe on the Juniata above Lewistown

problem of migration will be solved and that a new shad run will again come to Susquehanna and Juniata waters.

Since life in the Juniata is so abundant and easily seen, this river tells us something about all Pennsylvania waters. Ecological cycles, the food chain, and all the life of the waterway are bound up together in a complex and delicate system. The heron or muskellunge depend on minnows and crayfish, which depend on mayflies and caddisflies, which depend on algae that we think of as weeds. Metals or chemicals ingested by a caddisfly are ingested by us when we have fish for dinner. While many streams are damaged and unable to support a healthy community of plants and animals, all of them once did, and life could return to many waters as it has in the Juniata.

The Upper Susquehanna:
A River with History

Because of its massive size, the Susquehanna is generally thought of in three parts: the wild West Branch, draining central and north central Pennsylvania, the upper river, or "North Branch," and the main stem, from the two branches' confluence at Sunbury to the Chesapeake Bay. Among other rivers of the nation, the Susquehanna ranks twelfth in average flow. The upper river is wide and winding—big, open waters with gentle riffles, pleasant scenery of farms and mountains, riverfront towns, and excellent warm-water fishing. Smallmouth bass, walleye, and muskellunge are plentiful. Several tributaries offer exciting and difficult whitewater paddling in the high flows of springtime: Sugar Creek, Towanda Creek, Schrader Branch of Towanda Creek, Wyalusing Creek, Tunkhannock Creek and its South Branch, Mehoopany Creek, and Bowman Creek.

A popular reach for lazy Susquehanna river traveling lies between Athens, near the New York border, and Tunkhannock, a small town thirty miles north of Scranton. "Tioga Point" was the earlier name for the narrow peninsula at Athens, the confluence of the Chemung and the Susquehanna. Here the rivers are dark brown, vile-looking but productive for fish. The Chemung, coming from the northwest, shows turbid evidence of Elmira and many farms. The Susquehanna originates in New York at Lake Otsega, "Glimmerglass" in the early American novels of James Fenimore

Cooper, then winds through scenic and pastoral hills, dips for thirty miles into Pennsylvania, bisects the Binghamton urban area, and then decidedly bends to the south. From Tioga Point down, water quality seems to gradually improve until the Lackawanna is reached.

Like the lower Juniata and upper Allegheny, Susquehanna shorelines are low and thickly tangled with vegetation. They are a prime wildlife habitat for often-seen herons, ducks, and shore birds. Unknowingly, we once camped beneath a great horned owl's nest, spotting the young predators late in the evening. To avoid disturbing the family more than we already had, we quickly got in our tents, while the mother sat on a distant limb, silhouetted in owlish seriousness, hooting as darkness grew.

High cliffs and rock outcrops add interest to the rolling landscape and offer good views. Best known of these are Wyalusing Rocks, just above Wyalusing and easily accessible from scenic Route 6. The wildest section of river lies below Mehoopany, as the Susquehanna drops over a sharp riffle, then wraps around a large and roadless bend, while even the railroad temporarily disappears into a tunnel. Lower sections from Wilkes-Barre to the West Branch confluence at Sunbury are more polluted, straighter, and less mountainous than the 100-mile reach in the northern counties of Bradford and Wyoming.

Etienne Brulé is largely unknown in American history, yet he was one of the great North American explorers and the first European to see much of the Susquehanna and Pennsylvania. The young Frenchman left no record of his travels and life among Indians, though a thread of his existence appears haphazardly in the writings of Champlain, Sagard, and Brébeuf. It was in 1610 that Brulé, working in Quebec under Samuel de Champlain, asked if he might winter with the Huron Indians to learn their language. Champlain agreed, and Brulé, probably eighteen years old, became the first European to travel the Ottawa and Mattawa rivers, to see Lake Nipissing and Georgian Bay, and to speak Huron. Eventually he would be the first white man to discover four of the five Great Lakes.

After aiding the Hurons against the Iroquois in 1609, the French initiated a long-lasting conflict. The significance of Brulé's involvement began in 1615, when Champlain and the Hurons were on their way southward to fight the Iroquois. Huron braves were selected to circle the southern territory and enlist aid from the Susquehannocks, allies of the Hurons from southern New York and northern Pennsylvania. Brulé sought permission to follow them, "to which I readily agreed," wrote Champlain, "since he was drawn thereto of his own inclination, and by this means would see their country and could observe the tribes that inhabit it." The mission proved unsuccessful, as the Susquehannock aid arrived at Champlain's prearranged meeting place only to discover that the Onondaga Nation of Iroquois had already defeated the combined French and Huron forces. In a

Opposite: Susquehanna below Sayre

pattern that he later adopted for life, Brulé chose not to return to Champlain's party and traveled southward with the Indians, beginning his two-year Susquehanna voyage.

Champlain later wrote of Brulé's journey:

> He employed himself in exploring the country visiting neighboring nations and lands and in passing the length of a river which discharges on the coast of Florida. The climate is very temperate and there are a great number of animals and game to be hunted. But to travel this country one must have great patience, for difficulties are to be met in its wilderness. And he continued as far as the sea along this river, past islands in it and lands that border it, which are inhabited by several nations and many savage peoples. And after he had traversed the country and discovered what was noticeable he returned to Carantouan.

In a feat of early exploration, Brulé followed the river from New York to the Chesapeake Bay (mistaken for the coast of Florida) and back again. Some historians have speculated that he may also have poled up the West Branch to the present site of Muncy. Throughout 1615 and 1616, Brulé

Foam in the Susquehanna below Towanda

passed Tioga Point, Standing Stone, Wyalusing Rocks, a crystal-clear Lack-awanna, an expansive West Branch confluence, rapids full of migrating shad at York Haven, and the great falls where Conowingo Dam now sits. A lone white man, aided only by primitive equipment, he cruised the length of a great river and back again. John Smith received credit for discovering the Susquehanna in 1608, though he sailed only to the mouth of the river and took one look at the rapids below Conowingo Falls, declaring them unnavigable. After Brulé's voyage, over 100 years elapsed before the first settlers arrived.

The upper river is best known in history for revolutionary war battles in the Wyoming Valley of Luzerne County and for the Yankee-Pennamite Wars, resulting from dual land claims by the colonies of Pennsylvania and Connecticut.

Before the borders of the colonies were definitely established and agreed upon, Pennsylvanians thought the upper Susquehanna and Lackawanna valleys belonged to them, dating from a 1736 sale by the Indians to Thomas and Richard Penn, and later by a 1768 deed that was drafted at Fort Stanwix, New York. Meanwhile the Connecticut Susquehanna Company was formed as the first great real-estate brokerage for the region. In 1754 it executed a treaty with the Iroquois nations, gaining yet another title to land known as the Wyoming Valley. It is likely that the Indians never intended the land to be deeded, in the English sense of the word, but rather conceived of a proposition by which land would be shared. Ambiguous royal grants also complicated the situation. New Englanders poured into the area in 1763, and with firm

Homemade raft, the Susquehanna above Towanda

occupancy, questions of colonial ownership had to wait until after the Revolutionary War. The heritage of Yankee settlers can be seen today in the distinct New England architectural styles that are common across the northern tier of Pennsylvania, extending south to the village of Picture Rocks on Muncy Creek and to the town of Muncy.

During this era the upper Susquehanna and its West Branch valley were frontier regions and as such became the target of Indian attacks, which were supplied and incited by the British. In 1778, while Washington's revolutionary army was occupied elsewhere, 400 British and 700 Iroquois embarked from Tioga Point, landed at Bowman Creek below Tunkhannock, and crossed the mountains to Wyoming Valley. The New England colonists were led by Zebulon Butler and the fanatical Lazarus Stewart, who had instigated the Paxtang Boys' killing of peaceful Indian families near Lancaster in the "Conestoga Massacre." Leaving their fort, the Yankees attacked the stronger force and lost half their men. This became known as the second Wyoming Massacre (the first having taken place in 1763) and signaled the "Big Runaway"—a movement of nearly all frontier settlers down the rivers to safety. As word of the fighting spread southward and up to the West Branch, frontier farmers packed what they could onto rowboats, rafts, and tied-together logs and drifted with the current to white settlements below.

Counterattacks came, as colonial armies followed river routes into Iroquois and British-occupied country. Thomas Hartley led 200 men from

Photo by John Lazenby

Susquehanna at Towanda

Muncy, up Lycoming Creek, down Towanda and Sugar creeks to Tioga. Then a major expedition to recapture lands and to break Indian resistance was directed by General John Sullivan. With 3,500 men and 2,000 pack horses the army walked north, sometimes wading deep into the Susquehanna. They camped at the Lackawanna River, Wyalusing, Sheshequin, and Tioga Point. James Clinton built 200 bateaux at Otsega Lake, dammed the outlet to collect a head of water, then destroyed the dam and rode the flood crest toward Tioga Point, where he combined forces with Sullivan. Without contest, the army marched north and west, destroying Iroquois villages and crops through the upper Susquehanna and Genessee basins. General William T. Sherman is generally credited with developing burned-landscape warfare as he crossed Georgia in 1864, but Sullivan perfected the style nearly 100 years earlier. After the Revolution, Pennsylvanians and Connecticuters turned to fighting one another until land claims were finally settled.

Much history has touched the upper Susquehanna. French Azilum was a colony begun in 1793 along the western shore, south of Towanda near Standing Stone. Two hundred fugitives from the French Revolution lived here, intending to bring Marie Antoinette. They traveled up the river in Durham boats and built fifty log cabins, including a sixty-by-eighty-foot, 2½-story log mansion for the Queen and Dauphin, who were unable to escape from France. An Azilum corporation is now attempting to reconstruct parts of the settlement.

Several songs of Stephen Foster deal with the upper Susquehanna, the "Tioga Waltz" and "Camptown Races," which were annually run at the small village of Camptown northeast of Wyalusing. The Susquehanna Canal was constructed along these reaches, and remains can be found in many areas.

History along the river has recorded the boom and bust of anthracite coal in the Scranton, Wilkes-Barre, and Hazelton regions. In the late 1960s, conflict raged over the planned construction of an experimental fast-breeder nuclear reactor near Tunkhannock. Though they faced a long and seemingly hopeless struggle, local residents who opposed the development succeeded in stopping the nuclear project. Downriver, at Berwick, a different nuclear reactor is now being built, but still contested.

The greatest of all American storms, Hurricane Agnes, caused flooding over much of the northeast in June 1972. Nowhere was the damage greater than in Wilkes-Barre, where the Susquehanna overtopped the city dikes. Damages to the Wyoming Valley area were estimated at over $2 billion; 80,000 people were temporarily displaced and 20,000 lost their homes. Flooding of the city began when water breached sections of the dike that had subsided over coal mines. Along with Johnstown, Wilkes-Barre illustrates the false sense of security created by flood-control structures.

Penetrating the Scranton urban area and meeting the Susquehanna between this city and Wilkes-Barre, the Lackawanna River is slowly recovering from the frenzied abuse of consecutive timber, iron, and coal eras. Mine drainage, sewage, and industrial wastes remain a problem, but the stream has improved, with new waterfront parks at Scranton and Mayfield. A springtime canoe regatta, sponsored annually by the Chamber of Commerce and the Luzerne-Lackawanna Environmental Council, draws support for the river and for preserving it. Except for the Pocono headwaters, the river does not meet water-quality standards for swimming. Someday, though, the Lackawanna could shine as a success in river reclamation.

Because of the natural, historical, and recreational values of the upper Susquehanna, designation of the river in the state scenic-river system is being sought by the Save the Endless Mountains Association, a citizens' organization that is active in a five-county region.

Susquehanna Basin River Sketches

Sinnemahoning Creek

Sinnemahoning is a major stream system of north central Pennsylvania. Its three main branches—Driftwood, Bennett, and First Fork—form the largest West Branch Susquehanna tributary. Thousands of acres are wild and unpopulated, though many southern and western regions have been strip mined.

Bennett is the largest branch and also the most affected by mine acid. Beginning near DuBois, the stream flows north and east, joined by polluted tributaries but also by clean trout waters like Medix Run. Fish are

The old Commercial Hotel along the Sinnemahoning, village of Driftwood

Trout fisherman, Driftwood Branch, Sinnemahoning Creek below Emporium

nearly nonexistent in Bennett Branch, and though orange precipitate or "yellow boy" stains the bed, views of the creek from Route 555 are very scenic, and canoe travel is excellent through early and mid springtime. There is little development along the stream, as the acid waters have never attracted fishermen. Riffles are Class I, with several fast rocky sections.

Driftwood Branch begins northeast of Saint Marys, flows through Emporium, and parallels Route 120 to the village of Driftwood, where it meets Bennett Branch. Driftwood is cleaner and still improving, with good fishing along much of its length. From Emporium or Cameron down, this makes an excellent but easy canoe voyage in high and medium-high waters of March, April, and sometimes May. The finest section is a series of wide bends below the village of Sterling Run.

First Fork is the smallest of three Sinnemahoning branches, but includes the best fishing waters. Thousands of anglers converge on the First Fork and its East Fork at the beginning of trout season. Clear waters drift through wide meadows and willow thickets with steep-sloped mountains of the north central highlands as a continual backdrop. Trailers and low-cost hunting and fishing cabins are scattered across many of the abandoned valley farms and crowd the banks of the stream, especially below Stevenson Dam.

The main stem of the Sinnemahoning is a wide, gentle stream that would be called a river in any other part of the country but Pennsylvania. Route 120 and a railroad parallel its shores, but much of the waterfront is still undisturbed. It is especially scenic below the mouth of the First Fork. This is an excellent beginner's canoe trip, with an easy take-out at Keating bridge, just before the West Branch of the Susquehanna.

Pennsylvania's only elk herd lives in the Sinnemahoning basin. This region also has an interesting history, which includes the notorious logging era of the late 1800s and tales about a legendary boatload of gold bullion that disappeared while being shipped downriver during the Civil War. It won't hurt to scratch around your camp site if you canoe the Sinnemahoning!

Little Pine Creek

Little Pine is the largest tributary to Pine Creek, entering at Waterville, which is near the lower end of the National Scenic River Study. North central forests and farmland feed water to Little Pine through a valley of unusual charm and scenic appeal. Origins of the stream lie near the town of Liberty. Pollution from a milk processing plant has been a problem here, and small amounts of acid mine drainage enter below the village of English Center, but overall water quality is excellent.

Unlike the steep and narrow gorge of Pine Creek, this valley stretches as a flat expanse, a half mile in width. Mountains border its edges, and clear water angles back and forth through rapids and pools. Little Pine is an almost unknown canoeing waterway. Its sharp bends, narrow chutes, and sudden drops make English Center to Little Pine Dam an excellent and exciting run when the flow is at high level. Thousands of fishermen come here in April. The stream and reservoir are heavily stocked, but high water temperatures will not support a year-round population of trout. A state park is maintained at the impoundment, eight miles north of Waterville, though the dam may become best known for its inordinate load of silt. The project is less than thirty years old, and mud has nearly filled the lake area to its summer pool elevation. The cost of removing the silt is prohibitive. Ironically, the flood-control dam was filled to capacity eight hours before the crest of the Hurricane Agnes flood of 1972; at the highest point of discharge, water simply entered one end of the impoundment and flowed out of the other, providing little or no flood mitigation to downstream communities.

Little Pine Creek Reservoir, with accumulation of silt

Sunrise, Little Pine Creek below English Center

Lycoming Creek

Flowing due south to the Susquehanna's West Branch, Lycoming Creek shows many contrasts of Pennsylvania. Headwaters begin on rolling dairy farms. The creek passes Roaring Branch and Ralston, small villages with wooden frame buildings typical of old-time mining and lumber towns. High slopes with rocky outcrops confine a scenic valley. Below Trout Run village, the creek passes a final gap in the Allegheny Front, leaving the northern plateau and gorge country for a gentler West Branch Valley. Here, with closely paralleling highways, development crowds the creek. Seasonal homes and cabins have been converted to year-round residences, trailer parks have multiplied, and commercial development of Route 15 spreads erratically. In spite of this, many scenic reaches of lower Lycoming

First day of trout season, Lycoming Creek at Fields Station

still remain. At Heshbon Cliffs, rocky faces and old hemlocks rise from the western bank. A relocation of Route 15 is likely to cross this area.

Lycoming Creek offers very good fishing, though excavation of flood-deposited gravel has affected lower reaches. Whitewater canoeing is excellent, with exciting Class II rapids in upper sections that can be run only during high water. Tight bends and fallen timber demand fast maneuvering.

Highlighting the basin is the scenic tributary, Rock Run. Flowing fifteen miles from Ellenton to Ralston, this crystalline stream reveals pools swirled in deep green, with rapids and small falls. Miners Run is another, smaller tributary to Rock Run, dropping from the northern mountainside in many waterfalls. Nearly all of Rock Run is on state forest land; however, mineral rights in upper reaches remain in private ownership. "Natural" and "wild" area status under state forest management has been considered to gain protection for the stream banks, but neither designation has been enacted.

Tioga River

Flowing north from Pennsylvania to New York are the Tioga, Genesee, and Allegheny rivers. While the Genesee becomes a major tributary to Lake Ontario and then the St. Lawrence, the Allegheny returns to Pennsylvania in Kinzua Dam. The Tioga joins a broad, muddy Chemung, again flowing south to the Susquehanna at Tioga Point or Athens, Pennsylvania. Though the Tioga is a large stream draining 461 square miles, it is not well-known outside the local area. Mine acid infects the river from its headwaters near Arnot and Morris Run. Deep mining was extensive; tunnels were dug into the mountains, which now discharge thousands of gallons of acid water. Modern strip-mining techniques may be reclaiming some of these areas by reexcavating the mines, then backfilling to minimize the amount of water that flows into acid-bearing shales.

During high springtime runoff, exciting whitewater flows above Blossburg and downstream toward Covington. After that, the river is slower and closely paralleled by Route 15. Efforts to remove flood-deposited gravel and to dike sections of riverbank have resulted in extensive bulldozing. A dam is under construction near the town of Tioga by the Army Corps of Engineers. Waters will be impounded for ten miles, while an adjacent dam will flood a portion of Crooked Creek, a Tioga tributary. Landslides have plagued construction efforts, though the completed reservoirs should provide flood protection to the downstream communities of Corning and Elmira. As a separate effort, the Soil Conservation Service has prepared a nonstructural flood control plan—the first of its kind to be proposed by that agency.

Towanda Creek

Most tributaries to the upper Susquehanna, or the portion above the mouth of the West Branch, are fairly short. Exceptions to this are the Chemung, which is primarily a New York river, the highly polluted Lackawanna, which flows through Carbondale and Scranton, Tunkhannock Creek, Fishing Creek, and Towanda Creek.

Towanda's watershed rises near Canton and enters the Susquehanna through broad, swampy wetlands below Towanda. Route 414 is a scenic drive through this agricultural valley, with rolling dairy farms, highland ridges to the south, and frequent evidence of glacial activity which scoured northern Pennsylvania years ago. Fishing is good, and canoeing includes a mixture of fast and gentle current, but only during high water.

The Schrader Branch of Towanda Creek is a highlight. Covering over one-third of the basin, most of this stream is within state game lands. An abandoned railroad right-of-way follows a wooded Schrader Valley as the stream twists and plunges. This is one of the few wild reaches of stream in Pennsylvania that has no road or railroad for ten miles or longer. Water quality and trout fishing are outstanding.

Penns Creek

In the central Pennsylvania country of high northeastward-pointing ridges and spacious agricultural valleys, the basin of Penns Creek includes 554 square miles. Rising in Penns Cave near Potters Mills and State College, it flows eastward past Coburn, Weikert, Laurelton, and the hamlet of Penns Creek, where Walnut Acres—a well-known organic farm and natural foods store—is located. The stream forms a western boundary of the Isle of Que, which is a long peninsula in the mile-wide Susquehanna near Selinsgrove.

Waters of lower Penns Creek often run muddy; however, the quality of its upper reaches is excellent. Vast deposits of limestone and cool spring waters make this a productive and popular trout fishery. Public acquisition of a railroad right-of-way between Coburn and Weikert has complemented state forest holdings along the stream, offering a scenic hiking trail with fishing access. Rock climbers from Penn State University also use this area, visiting a rugged set of cliffs near Coburn. Canoeing on Penns Creek is possible in early spring, but since this is a favorite stream of many fishermen, it's best to float other waters after the opening of trout season in mid April.

Penns Creek below Poe Paddy State Park

Stony Creek

Stony Creek has become known as the closest wild valley to Harrisburg and southeast population centers of the Commonwealth. Waters flow for thirty miles between Second Mountain and Stony Mountain, meeting the Susquehanna at Dauphin, only twelve miles north of the state capital. Though the basin area is only thirty-six square miles, the upper two-thirds has no public roads or vehicular access. Clean waters cross small riffles, then deep pools that offer excellent trout fishing. Heavy cobbles nearly always cover the bottom—water-worn sandstone from paralleling mountain ridges. The area has been popular with thousands of fishermen and hunters. Backpackers now hike in Stony Creek Valley, and hundreds of bicyclists use an old road that is closed to motor vehicles.

Stony Creek near the site of a proposed pump-storage reservoir project

The upper basin was protected as state game lands in the 1960s; how-ever, 1,700 acres of Stony Creek Valley were traded to the Pennsylvania Power and Light and Metropolitan Edison companies for 5,400 road-accessible acres in neighboring Clark Creek Valley. PP&L plans to construct a reservoir for electric power generation through pump storage—a process whereby water would be pumped from a Stony Creek impoundment to a secondary reservoir on top of the mountain, then dropped from the higher storage area to generate power at peak periods, or times when demand for electricity is greatest.

Opponents to the project have been vocal, numerous, and effective. Led by the Stony Creek Valley Coalition, they include many major conservation and environmental groups. They charge that Stony is the last remaining wild valley of southeastern Pennsylvania, that its values are irreplaceable, that the pump storage project is inefficient, and that the game lands should not have been traded in the first place. Nevertheless, PP&L plans to pro-ceed, though it has delayed development activities. Many questions remain to be resolved before construction will begin, if ever. In 1978 study was initiated for the state scenic-river designation, which would probably stop the dam.

Conestoga Creek

Much of southeastern Pennsylvania drains toward the Susquehanna through Swatara, Conewago, Conestoga, Pequea, and Octoraro creeks. This rich agricultural belt has been one of the most productive farming regions in the world.

Conestoga is the best-known stream, drifting past the historic city of Lan-caster. A canal operated along Conestoga, and the remains of locks can be seen. More than anything else, the Conestoga wagon has made this a famil-iar name. The large, canvas-covered "prairie schooners" were invented and originally built in the area, then sold to settlers during the early westward movement.

Yellow and muddy with Lancaster County runoff, Conestoga exemplifies many of the farmland creeks. A Pennsylvania State University report esti-mates that twelve tons of soil are lost each year from an average agricul-tural acre.

Warm-water fish such as bass, suckers, carp, and catfish can be caught in the Conestoga. Canoeists can make a pleasant trip on medium or high waters from Lancaster to a park near Safe Harbor Power Plant on the Susquehanna. Several short portages are necessary.

The Ohio Basin

The Allegheny:
River of Northwestern Pennsylvania

Rainfall from northwestern Pennsylvania flows to New Orleans, and the entire path could have been called Allegheny. This river is larger than the Monongahela where they join to form the Ohio. The Ohio, in turn, carries twice the volume of the Mississippi at Cairo, where the two megarivers meet. Thus if one were to begin in the Gulf of Mexico and journey northward by always following the larger fork of the stream, one would eventually reach Coudersport in Potter County. As it happened, different names were selected for this single massive waterway. The French labeled the Mississippi, Ohio, and Allegheny from Indian dialects, which are translated as "Great River," "Beautiful River," and "Fair Waters."

The Allegheny flows gently for 314 miles to Pittsburgh. Walleye, muskellunge, northern pike, and smallmouth bass make it a popular warm-water fishery. It is a large river, attractive to canoeists, campers, and just about everybody. Brady's Bend is one of its landmarks, complete with historical marker and twenty-five-cent telescopes. Art festival visitors go swimming at Kennerdale, Boy Scouts flock to camp near Tionesta, a national forest welcomes campers at Buckaloons, motorboaters launch into Kinzua Reservoir, and deer hunters migrate to the McKean and Potter county headwaters.

Like the Delaware, its upstream reaches bear no resemblance to the lower urban ones. Industry and highways monopolize water frontage near Pittsburgh in a blanketed way that compares only to the Monongahela, Ohio, Schuylkill, and tidal Delaware. A series of nine dams and locks step upward to New Kensington and Kittanning, drawing barges of the Mississippi and Ohio to the north and the rural core of Pennsylvania. Parts of the lower river are being restored to an undevastated condition. The Western Pennsylvania Conservancy is acquiring wooded islands, and opportunities for public access to the water are improving.

If one were to segregate the Allegheny of northern Pennsylvania from the rest of the river, East Brady could be the boundary. Here, seventy-two miles above the Ohio River, the backwater of dam number nine stops, and one can see a smooth, winding current. Without a navigation channel, the industrial conglomeration of the waterfront terminates and only reappears

Opposite: Potter County Courthouse and the Allegheny flood channel, Coudersport

Sunrise and Labrador Retriever, Allegheny River
near Franklin

at sporadic intervals. Emlenton lies twenty-one miles upstream, and thousands of canoeists and fishermen use a thirty-five-mile section that reaches farther northward to Franklin. Cottages and cabins are scattered here and elsewhere on the middle and upper Allegheny, as the current weaves in distended coiling bends. Green herons nest by the dozens in a riverine cover of willows and birch. Yellow sneezeweed colors the shorelines in August, and wet-rooted, white-flowered "lizards tail" blurs the boundary of water and land, blooming in a profligacy that rivals the dandelions of my backyard. Kennerdale is a village and cabin complex where an art and music festival is held each August. Here 3,140 acres of the west shore have been acquired by the Commonwealth for Allegheny State Park, but no facilities have been developed.

In the 1830s a canal was constructed up French Creek, a tributary that meets the Allegheny at Franklin, the site of historic Fort Venango. French Creek Canal was the ultimate in poor planning, as there wasn't enough water to float a boat. The dry canal, however, represented the beginnings of a more ambitious idea—an inland commercial waterway from Lake Erie to Pittsburgh, with "an escalation of poor planning," as one local critic said. In 1919 the Allegheny River Improvement Association was formed to promote advancement of locks and dams upstream from Pittsburgh and to support a route of commerce to the Great Lakes.

A similar proposal was advanced for canal construction from the port
city of Ashtabula on Lake Erie to the industrialized Ohio River via Youngstown, New Castle, and the Beaver River. The project has been criticized for
its projected cost, farmland consumption, resident displacement, and ecological impact on streams and Lake Erie. The benefactors would be industries along the way, primarily in Youngstown. It was known as "Mike's
Ditch" after Michael Kirwan of Ohio, senior member of the U.S. House
Appropriations Committee. Kirwan supported it, while freshman Representative Joseph Vigorito of Pennsylvania objected, saying the project included "cynically juggled figures to justify an indefensible boondoggle," yet
in 1968 it gained the credibility of $2 million in planning funds.

The more eastern Allegheny Canal route attracted renewed attention
after Kirwan ended his last term in office. Through the project, industrial
traffic would be extended above dam number nine at Brady's Bend,
through Emlenton to Franklin, and then up French Creek to Erie. The
canal was long regarded as the primary reason for opposition to National
Scenic River designation of the Allegheny, protection that would prohibit
canal construction within the designated reach.

While the canal has been a threat so unlikely and long-debated that few
people get excited any more, dredging of sand and gravel from the middle
and upper Allegheny was an issue that exploded statewide in 1974.

For years commercial operators had been dredging sections of the river
above Oil City. When temporary permit extensions were granted in 1972,
the Pennsylvania Department of Environmental Resources included three
stipulations under the Dams and Encroachments Act and Clean Streams
Act: dredging was prohibited within fifty feet of shorelines, during weekends or holidays, and in natural or undisturbed areas. Operators appealed
the restrictions, raising questions that were not resolved until 1976. Opponents of dredging sought to eliminate all mining from the river, stating
that land-based sand and gravel should be extracted. A United States Fish
and Wildlife Service report recommended a phase-out of dredging, identifying what many people recognized as obvious: game-fish populations in
natural reaches of the river were far superior to those in disturbed areas.
The study also counted sixty-nine species of fish, three of which are en-
dangered in the state. Regional benefits of a $113 million recreational
economy were regarded by fishing and recreation interests to be far more
significant than those of river excavation. Pennsylvania's Federation of
Sportsman's Clubs supported the dredgers' fight, saying that no permanent
harm to the river would result from continuing to dredge. The Department of Transportation, largest purchaser of gravel, testified in support of
the sand and gravel companies.

A newly formed Allegheny River Protective Association worked to restrict the dredging, but statewide attention was not apparent until introduction of House Bill 685, proposed legislation that would have eliminated the
Department of Environmental Resources' authority to deny or adequately

regulate river-based mining operations. Reaction was incensed from all corners of the Commonwealth, as this bill was not limited to the Allegheny but included waters throughout the state. Environmentalists became active in fighting the "Allegheny River dredging bill," a measure that ultimately passed the House, where Representative John Ladaddio had sponsored it, but not the Senate.

In 1976, when the heat of controversy subsided, the Department published a new policy and new regulations. A five-year phase-out of all dredging above East Brady was announced and praised by river enthusiasts. The waterway was clearly recognized as a significant natural resource: "No other stream in northwestern Pennsylvania has the recreational and fishery value of the Upper Allegheny." The Department's position was greatly enhanced by national and state scenic-river systems. DER stated: "The Upper Allegheny River . . . has been named as a potential addition to the National Wild and Scenic Rivers System, under proposed Federal legislation, and has been designated for in-depth study as a highest priority river under the Pennsylvania Wild and Scenic Rivers program."

Both the canal and dredging issues have stimulated support for the scenic-river programs. Federal designation would prohibit the use of federal funds for the canal, and the mere potential for designation helped the state adopt a policy against dredging. In 1968 the entire river from Kinzua Dam (built before the Wild and Scenic Rivers Act was considered) to Pittsburgh was recommended for federal study by Congressman John Saylor, but upper Allegheny Representative Albert Johnson deleted his section, leaving only the industrial flatwater below East Brady. The lower Allegheny study attained notoriety as the easiest one that the Bureau of Outdoor Recreation ever did. One glance told them that the river was ineligible because of pollution, dams, and development. The federal agency went through the motions, however, and in 1973 produced a thirty-two-page report, which significantly recommended another study, the same one originally intended by Saylor. "As a result of the feasibility investigation, it is recommended that the Upper Allegheny, between East Brady and Kinzua Dam, be considered for future in-depth study to determine whether it qualifies for inclusion in the National Wild and Scenic Rivers System."

Armed with an official report, Paul Bohlander, Lud Haller, and other members of the Protective Association gained support from Senators Hugh Scott and Richard Schweiker. George Reese of Greenville testified before a Senate committee in 1975, pointing out the recreational values of the river and the pressures that threatened them.

The state Department of Environmental Resources also supported a bill that would authorize federal study of the Allegheny. A 1974 comment of the governor was repeated: "I would like to recommend that the upper section of the river, from Kinzua Dam to East Brady, be included for future study for possible designation in the National Wild and Scenic Rivers System."

Deputy Secretary Clifford McConnell of the Department also referred to the state planning report, "Outdoor Recreation Horizons": "Those guidelines are explicit in support of the National Wild and Scenic Rivers Act and identify this particular river segment as a potential candidate for detailed study."

Resistance came from Representative Johnson and from local economic interests, such as the Warren County Chamber of Commerce. "This three-year study is a narrow, one-shot deal and would practically paralyze all activities on and along the river for the duration of the study," the congressman said.

"In fact," Protective Association spokesman Reese replied, "the study would only place a moratorium on federal funds for water resource projects, such as the canal." The next election saw the congressman soundly defeated. In 1978 the National Parks and Recreation Act authorized a study of the upper Allegheny for the national rivers system.

Allegheny River below West Hickory

Below Kinzua the Allegheny has two exceptionally scenic areas: the thirty-five-mile reach between Franklin and Emlenton, and fifty miles of river from Buckaloons to Oil City. While great falcated bends characterize the lower and shorter reach, the more northern passage is uncommonly rich in islands. This is a favorite section of the Allegheny, for here are many rivers in a maze of miniature, convoluted channels. Travelers are drawn into

Allegheny River near Oil City

wooded backwaters and a mystery of twisting riffles that flatten into maple-crowded pools. Turtles as big as serving platters lie on sun-warmed rocks, great blue herons wade into the shallows, and kingfishers rattle their call from one bank to the next. The islands offer a liberty of separation from other lands and people. They are a world apart, and you can relax in confidence that no trucks or locomotives will run you down. Euell Gibbons called an island "a small body of land surrounded by the need for a boat."

As in the Susquehanna below Sunbury, islands are everywhere, a result of the river's tireless energy in clutching soil fragments from above, carrying them downward in a brown current, then dropping the oozing earth in quiet eddies. Like drifting snow, watery lands continually change; more soil settles on leeward sides, while floods rip at the upper extremities. Long and slender forms have outgrown themselves when high water rattles the brush and breaks into the land, digging one spot, then consuming another, eventually bursting forth on the opposite side. The land is split, and afterward the incision may grow deeper. As a constricted passage, the new channel may trap unearthed trees and the infinite assortment of debris that floats in a flood. Keelboat and steamboat pilots had names for all the islands: Brokenstraw, Clark's, Thompson's, Steward, Charley Smith's Bars, Mill Stone, Goose Flat, McGee's Bar, Courson, Maguyer's Bar, Tidioute, White Oak, Hemlock, Hickory Town, and many more.

"Islands are a highlight of the Allegheny," said John Oliver, president of the Western Pennsylvania Conservancy, a private, nonprofit conservation organization that has done remarkable work to protect sections of the Youghiogheny, Slippery Rock Creek, and this river. Recognizing the waterway's vast importance, the Conservancy has undertaken a task that only it could effectively accomplish. David Fahringer, a noted landscape architect, was hired to prepare a comprehensive study of the riverine corridor, identifying scenic, wild, or recreationally valuable areas. Then, with a technique that had matured over many years, the Pittsburgh-based organization launched an effort to buy selected lands of the Allegheny.

Crulls Island was acquired and later resold to the federal government as an addition to Allegheny National Forest. "We're also acquiring vacant shorelines, adjacent hillsides, and access areas for boaters and fishermen," said Oliver. "The Allegheny represents one of the most significant features in the natural heritage of western Pennsylvania, and our goal is to save what we can of the remaining undeveloped lands." Usually the Conservancy resells its newly acquired property to a state or federal agency, which agrees to protect the land. So far 6,500 acres have been secured as open space.

In 1977, 1,355 Allegheny acres were protected in a way that exemplifies the Conservancy's importance and unique role. The Forest Service owned seven acres of commercial real estate in Radnor, near Philadelphia. Originally the site was intended to become a new Forest Service headquarters, plans which the government later dropped. By law the Forest Service cannot sell land, but exchanges of property are allowed. After two years of negotiating, the Conservancy acquired five parcels of Allegheny River frontage, traded them for the seven commercial acres that were appraised at a similar value, then sold the commercial land to a tennis-court developer. This recovered the original Allegheny investment, which again jingled in the Conservancy's pocket, burning a hole for another sandy bank with silver maples.

The Western Pennsylvania Conservancy's acquisition program may be an important indicator of changing trends and strategies in open-land preservation and recreational development. The river has been recognized as a focus, and efforts are made to preserve pieces of shoreline, scattered as they might be. Clearly this differs from the "buy-and-build-a-park" technique that was more common for many years. The new approach incorporates several important features:

It is based on the riverine environment rather than on establishing a consolidated management unit where access and activity can be tightly controlled. By securing key sections of riverway, environmental protection and water-oriented recreational objectives may be best accomplished, since these lands are the most fragile and also the most desirable for leisure-time activities. A project is likely to be regional in scope, crossing many counties and involving different kinds of landscapes and communities.

The final result will be a patchwork of publicly and privately owned lands, not a solid "block of green" on the map. Public ownership will be important for access, recreational sites, natural areas, and wild lands. Otherwise, private use will prevail, probably with local zoning and flood-plain regulations. Efforts are long-term, reflecting the complexity, the lack of condemnation powers, and the broad goals of the programs.

Legal action such as scenic-river designation may be sought to protect the river—a much larger resource than a park. Many difficult questions are involved: Is a dam needed for flood control, water supply, or hydroelectric generation? Is a canal feasible and in the best interest? The river, in essence, *is* the park, and there are frequent conflicts regarding its most appropriate use.

Recreation is not regarded as an independent activity but as a total experience. It incorporates a variety of skills and interests, such as camping, canoeing, fishing, outdoor cooking, hiking, nature study, and photography. It is not dependent on one particular site but upon a high-quality natural environment. It can involve many degrees of social togetherness from solitary wilderness to a group outing.

Cost alone has become a major deterrent to many conventional programs of park acquisition and recreation facility development. Construction and maintenance are very expensive. To buy large blocks of land is difficult, not to speak of the hostility and objections that accompany the threat of condemnation. "One favorable aspect of an inflationary economy is that it benefits the natural environment, and all government agencies must now recognize this," Oliver said. "To establish a river protection and recreation program, only inexpensive facilities need to be developed, and a relatively small percentage of shoreline may be essential for public acquisition." With the Western Pennsylvania Conservancy and with the access and open-space

Industrial discharge, Allegheny River at Emlenton

programs of the Pennsylvania Department of Environmental Resources, the United States Forest Service, and the Pennsylvania Game and Fish Commissions, many of our streams may remain available for public use.

Closer to the headwaters, Kinzua Dam formed northern Pennsylvania's longest impoundment in 1967 when it was hailed as an economic boon to northwestern counties and as a salvation to Pittsburgh through flood control. Recreation and flood reduction were the main purposes of the 180-foot dam, and it effectively provided both. The Flood Control Acts of 1936, 1938, and 1941 authorized the project, which had a 1.3 to 1.0 benefit-cost ratio: for every dollar spent, $1.30 would be returned. This was a close ratio, where at least a one-to-one comparison was needed for Congressional action. If the dam were being considered today, its construction would be questioned more seriously because of economics and escalated costs, environmental impact analysis, and perhaps most important, new social views.

The reservoir flooded a Seneca Indian Reservation given to Chief Cornplanter through the oldest treaty in the Congressional archives—an agreement that George Washington signed. The Seneca Nation would hold the lands "so long as the Allegheny flows and the sun and moon shine," the 1794 agreement read. Indians and their consultant, Arthur E. Morgan, argued that a better alternative to provide Pittsburgh's flood control was available. A legal battle ensued between the 482 Indians and the federal government, and while the court did not determine that the sun and moon would no longer shine, it was decided that the Allegheny would indeed cease to flow. Now the village sites of Jennesadaga and Kinzua are deep under watery brown silt.

After a long upstream journey from Pittsburgh, we finally enter the headwaters of the river that early French explorers called "La Belle Riviere." Steamboats once went as far as Salamanca and Olean, New York, where the river shrinks and shallow sand bars grow. In geologic history, the river once went north from Olean to Lake Erie, a route that became blocked by continental ice masses that forced the current into new paths southward. Similar reversals of flow happened at Warren and French Creek.

Rolling uplands of the basin are vastly different from the mountainous shorelines below, for this is hill-farming country, much of it now abandoned but showing many signs of past activity. Above Eldred the river penetrates deep woodlands of the "Allegheny Flats." Currents weave through a low, boglike forest that seems primeval in its wetness. With yearly floods, the flats have been unaffected by cabins and roads. This is the wildest part of the entire Allegheny, twisting in a serene monotony of miles. I've floated on the high waves of March when braids of river escape the muddy streambed and filter through the woods. Ponds lie everywhere, as lands behind the riverbank slope downward to the remains of ancient

Unloading at a campsite, upper Allegheny River

High water in the Allegheny flats below Port Allegany

channels. The phenomenon is unique to flatlands: when the stream is running bank-full, the canoeist can look *down* into the woods that lie at each side.

Like diagrams in geography books, meanders loop erratically, recurved upon themselves so that the traveler loses all accurate sense of direction. The river borders Port Allegany, called "Canoe Place" in earlier days. Here the long portage began—an Indian trail that connected waters of midland America to an eastern flow of the Sinnemahoning and Susquehanna. The river is drawn smaller, attenuated between sharp-cornered bends, and then Coudersport is bisected by a concrete channel that was created for flood protection. From there, an ascent begins toward the high divide of forest and farms where rainwater flows north to Lake Ontario, east toward the Chesapeake Bay, and southeast on a long voyage to the Gulf of Mexico.

Opposite: Clarion River below Ridgway

The Clarion: Clear Water Again?

It was one of those first springtime evenings. Warming us from a cold winter detachment, a breeze along the river carried the scent of soil, pine, and life. We sat on a flat rock that had been covered by high currents of early March and felt a new freshness as the last light of day glowed from ridges above. The Clarion churned mildly, just enough that the surface danced in watery agitation and most other sounds could be forgotten.

Behind us, on the road to Piney Dam, a sports car shifted down, coming to a stop. "It was a little too peaceful to last," Cindy said, as she turned to see what kind of company we had. Where a clearing had been cut along the banks of Deer Creek, just before it dumped a load of acid water into the river, the car was carefully parked. To our surprise, the hulking frame of Ken Linton, a limnologist from Clarion State College, emerged. He waved, smiled a little, and ambled toward us, stopping deliberately to peer into the stream in the manner of his trade. We had been friends for a while, and as the three of us talked, he turned stones, hunting a stonefly or a caddisfly nymph.

"There isn't a crawlin' thing in there," he concluded. "If you're looking for a sunset, you've found one, but I'm looking for life in that water, and there isn't any."

Linton agreed, however, that if you wanted to sit by a river, this was the only one. "This place is what keeps me going," he said a little later, as he

crawled back into the vehicle that seemed half his size, like the parson whose boots scuffled on the trail because his mule was too short. "It's got to be better. It can't go on like this. Right *there* is something that's got to be changed." He pointed to the orange-stained rocks, squinting seriously. Five years later, on the same beach where Cindy and I had enjoyed a spring evening, we loaded the canoe one morning for a twenty-mile cruise to the end of the river. At ten o'clock the water rose like a flash flood on the South Platte. Knowing that the release gates had been opened at Piney Hydroelectric Dam just upstream, we embarked from a glistening sand bar. As Ken Linton says, this reach of the Clarion is an ecological disaster with a pH of 4.0. Within this measure of acid or alkalinity, a rating of 6 or 7 would be normal. Lower scores mean more acid: a pH of 5 is the limit for keeping any fish alive. Piney Creek, Deer Creek, and Licking Creek pour their lifeless runoff from both sides; however, in all other respects, the lower river is a prize to the canoeist. Riffles are fast, and scenery is almost unmarred. For fifteen miles there are no roads or railroads.

We passed the proposed dam site near St. Petersburg. A 1969 Army Corps of Engineers' report calls for a structure nearly 300 feet high, which would impound waters for thirty miles to Cook Forest. Optimistically, the purposes are listed as "flood control, quality control, water supply, hydro-electric power, recreation, conservation, fish and wildlife enhancement, other environmental quality improvements, and economic development." Downstream groups such as the Three Rivers Improvement and Development Corporation in Pittsburgh have supported the dam, stating that it would have reduced flooding in June 1972 by three feet. Public benefits are claimed for industrial development of open space that lies downstream—lowlands of the Allegheny that now flood too frequently for private business to risk its investment. The Project Analysis report states, "In view of land now idle and potentially available for industrial develop-ment, flood plain regulation would not be an acceptable solution to the flood control problem." Fiscal conservatives and flood-plain management advocates objected, saying that it's one thing to claim benefits for protec-tion of *existing* development but quite another matter to list benefits for development of currently *vacant* land.

"The main problem is one of flood plain *development* control," says John Sweet of the American Canoe Association. "I don't agree that the public is to benefit from industrialization of flood plains and that tax dollars should be used to make these 'benefits' possible. Floods are a natural part of the life cycle along a river; if we don't want wet buildings, then we shouldn't build them there. Flood plains are less than five percent of the land—there are plenty of other places to go."

Economic development, however, has been a selling point, endorsed by the Appalachian Regional Commission and local individuals. Supporters of the reservoir recognized that cleaner water is a prerequisite for dam con-struction, and they began backing efforts to reduce mine drainage pollution. The Federal Water Resources Development Act of 1976 authorized a more detailed study of acid abatement for Clarion tributaries.

The lower eight miles of the river were especially enjoyable as it twisted in horseshoe bends with wild shorelines. Occasionally we could see evidence of coal stripping, but from the water one would never imagine the feverish activity that was taking place above. The return trip from Parker to Deer Creek by way of country roads seemed like a macabre tour of earthen surgery where the patient died. It occurred to me that the effect of coal mining on rivers is the inverse of urbanization. In mining country, uplands are ravaged, but the stream corridor is often untouched; with cities, the waterfront is the first land to be paved or industrialized, while highlands remain vacant. To pollute, both ways have been effective.

The troubles and values that I saw on the lower Clarion are reflected elsewhere along this 150-mile stream, but judging the rest of the watershed from these twenty miles would be like the blind man describing an elephant after feeling one leg. In Pennsylvania this is one of the major rivers and one of the most interesting.

The East Branch begins near Clermont and the West Branch near Mt. Jewett, high headwaters, as both names suggest. Similar streams run north to the Allegheny, west to Tionesta, or east to the many-branched forks of Sinnemahoning Creek, but these Clarion waters flow southward toward a confluence at Johnsonburg. The West Branch is the cleaner of the two, though chloride content, possibly from oil drilling, has been high in the past. Mine drainage runs into the East Branch, loading a small Army Corps dam with acid. Water quality has been improved through treatment at Bogardy Run and the covering of acid-bearing shales with soil. Sandstone that caps the upper Clarion basin is very high in acid content; thus a pH of 5 is possible on an undisturbed stream.

As if these problems weren't enough, evidence points to yet another: acid rainfall. "Northcentral Pennsylvania is in the rain shadow of Pittsburgh and midwestern industrial centers," says Ken Schoener of the Department of Environmental Resources, "and we know that acid content of the rain is increasing." Hydrochloric, nitric, and sulfuric acids are thought to stem primarily from gaseous, man-made pollutants such as sulfur dioxide and nitrogen oxides produced when burning fossil fuels. Prevailing winds sweep up these wastes of industry, power plants, and automobiles, while precipitation brings the odious elements earthward again. Maps have been drawn showing the acid content of rain; highest incidence in the nation is near Ithaca, New York, in a zone that includes much of northcentral Pennsylvania.

East and West branches meet at Johnsonburg, a small town with an old papermill. Downstream people used to ask, "Who can enjoy reading the *Saturday Evening Post* when we have to drink it too?" They were referring to the New York and Pennsylvania company's mill where the paper for the

Rapids of the Clarion near Hallton

Post was made. Effluent is pumped to the largest waste lagoon in the state, a lake of 400 acres or more. Different degrees of discharge have occurred in past years, prompting a series of state orders to clean up. Most recently, the Sierra Club filed legal action with effective results. "The mill seems generally to be in compliance with state regulations," a Department of Environmental Resources official from the Meadville office said. But there are days when the pulp mill smell still lingers with the river for twenty miles or more below Johnsonburg. Sewage wastes have been a major problem here and at Ridgway, six miles below, though secondary treatment is now effective in both towns.

Toby Creek is the largest tributary on the upper Clarion, churning through a wild gorge from Brockway but carrying a deadly load of acid, iron, and other residue from the mines. The Toby Creek Watershed Association has been active in reclamation efforts, and with continued involvement, theirs may be one of the better stories in stream improvement. Much of the lower creek is protected as State Game Lands.

Toby reaches the Clarion at Portland Mills, where a finer section of river begins. For eight miles the waterway is uninterrupted by roads or railroads, except for an old iron truss bridge at Arroyo. This area offers ideal camping for canoeists who run a three-day trip from Ridgway to Cook Forest on the high waters of springtime. Ledges rise from the shorelines with

Canoeing the Clarion below Cook Forest

clusters of aged pines. Rhododendron spreads everywhere, impenetrably tangled, leaves glistening in the rain or curling tightly in the frigid cold of winter.

Generally speaking, the Clarion has good riffles but few rapids, except for a drop five miles downstream of Hallton. The river transcends its peaceful character and plunges madly over deep, hidden boulders. On a cold, rainy morning in April, we beached above the whitewater for a good view, then ran the rapids through the center, our canoe pointing sharply up toward the sky and then down into the next trough.

Much of the western bank from Ridgway to Cooksburg is within Allegheny National Forest; with state parks, forests, and game lands, public open space comprises one-fourth of the stream's shoreline. Cook Forest is unquestionably the highlight. Many people are familiar with the Clarion from hiking cool, shaded trails of the state park. Aged pine and hemlock stand as one of the finest remnants of primeval woodland in Pennsylvania. Anthony Wayne Cook and A. Cook Sons Company had delayed the logging of over 6,000 acres until 1927, when a bill was signed by Governor John S. Fisher for $450,000 to acquire the virgin timber. Another $200,000 was needed and finally raised through public subscription and contributions. Boxes were placed in local schools, and in this way the pennies of children helped to preserve a magnificent eastern forest.

Strip mine

After investigating ninety miles of the Clarion, the federal Bureau of Outdoor Recreation reported in 1971 that the river did not meet National Wild and Scenic River standards. Water pollution from the paper mill, municipal sewage, and coal mines were listed as major problems, but the federal study added, "At such time as the water quality is improved to permit suitable outdoor recreation activities which are now precluded, the Clarion should be reconsidered for possible addition to the National System."

Spoil piles and erosion from strip mining, lower Clarion River

In reviewing the federal report, the governor of Pennsylvania expressed agreement: "I want to emphasize my interest in reconsidering the Clarion River in the future." Governor Milton Shapp also cited recent improvements to water quality, particularly on the East Branch.

Five years later, further advances were evident. "We've seen four-foot-long muskie," said Bob Cortez, a tough, likable, pollution-fighting patrolman for Pennsylvania's Fish Commission. "Rainbow trout and a twenty-two-inch walleye were caught at the Route 322 bridge," he added. "Cooksburg to Mill Creek is now a good fishery. A Commission survey found twenty-seven different types of minnows." Cortez feels that improvements at the paper mill have made a difference. "It's like the Juniata River—someday the Clarion will be just as well known for its recovery."

While there is less acid on the East Branch and upper Toby, pressure for mining has grown incredibly. "During 1970 I reviewed twelve or fifteen strip-mine applications," said Cortez. "In 1975 there were a hundred, and nearly all of them were approved." Out of 126 tributaries in Clarion County, only eight are suitable for fish stocking. "We fought to keep mining away from Beaver Creek and Turkey and Leatherwood, but Beaver's the only one we saved," he said. Ken Young of the Department of Environmental Resources' Meadville office reported receiving nearly 450 mine applications for the Clarion and Allegheny basins in one year.

A 1976 study showed 474 sources of acid in the Clarion watershed.

While much of the problem is from old abandoned mines, new ones also contribute. Strict enforcement of Pennsylvania regulations would minimize but not eliminate the problem. "But good enforcement's what we don't have," Cortez added. "I found weeds eighteen inches high where a siltation pond was required to be, and the inspector had been there only one week before."

Cortez stopped the car at Gravel Lick bridge, just below Cook Forest, and we walked down to look at the river. He pointed back over the ridge where lands above Maxwell Run were being stripped. "The best we can do is to try and save the clean streams we have left. That leaves plenty of choices for mining—118 out of 126 watersheds in the county!" Maxwell had been wild and unpolluted, an exception that may not last much longer. It was depressing, and there wasn't much else to say.

Cortez changed the subject. "You should see the canoes now—it's a beautiful river, and I just lean back on this bridge and laugh, the people who come down love it so much. I'd like to see national river designation; the scenery and fishing to Mill Creek are too good to change—let it be." But pressures for the St. Petersburg Dam could also arise again. "If there's money being spent to clean the Clarion, my guess is that a dam will go in," Cortez said. "It could provide for a lot of flatwater recreation." In addition to fifteen miles of wild river on the lower Clarion, the dam would flood ten miles between Cook Forest and Mill Creek, a section that is interrupted only by Gravel Lick bridge.

It was on this reach that the annual Clarion River Float began in 1970. Sponsored through an environmental education and action program at Clarion State College, the event was a river promotional effort in which 200 people cruised together. It would make the seeker of solitude shudder, but the event served effectively to bring attention to the waterway as a valuable resource. Prefloat publicity was intense, drawing canoeists from the local area and more distant places like Pittsburgh, Erie, Sharon, and State College. Free shuttle service was provided with pickup trucks, and information was distributed concerning the river and its problems. Two high school students won the trash collection contest; grating to a stop on the sandy Mill Creek beach, their canoe was top-heavy with an oil drum, three old tires, and miscellaneous cans rolling from bow to stern. Congressman John Saylor was there to express his regret that the Clarion was not yet in the National Rivers System.

It was like a celebration in many ways, with lots of happy people. There were original designs in water craft: five kids had three different sizes of inner tubes linked together, an American flag flew from the stern of one canoe, and a huge rubber duck was towed behind another. A golden retriever seemed to swim most of the way. While in a limited sense the float trip achieved little more than fun, it also represented a very significant turning point. For once the river was regarded as more than a route for floating logs to market, more than a wasteline for sewage, pulp debris, and acid, and more than a cause of flooding. The Clarion was recognized as a living river that can provide recreation and a special, essential kind of satisfaction. Use of the waterway will increase sharply over the coming years as trout return to many places above Mill Creek. Support for designation in the Pennsylvania Scenic Rivers System and in the National System will grow, but the Clarion's future is uncertain. These waters can show success, proving our ability to reclaim losses and preserve the best of Pennsylvania rivers. Or a history of abuse could repeat itself again.

The Clarion River below Cook Forest

Congestion of rafts, Swimmer's Rapid, Youghiogheny River

The Youghiogheny: Pennsylvania's Whitewater

Along with seventy-eight other folks, we took seats on the side of a black rubber raft. "Welcome to Whitewater Adventurers," the guide announced. "Today we're going to have a lot of fun on an eleven-mile float. There are lots of exciting rapids. First of all, we'll talk about your equipment. The most important thing is the life jacket. Put your arms through the holes and tie the straps in a knot—don't tie them in a bow." He spotted a misfit without seeming to hunt and pointed to a young girl. Embarrassed but determined, she was struggling with a tangle of straps, arm holes, and metal clips, trying to put the vest on upside down. "Better turn that jacket over; it'll float you feet-up that way." A friend offered some help.

"Okay, each raft should have four people, with the strongest two in back. Your paddles are the most dangerous thing, more dangerous than rocks or the water. Some people wave their paddles in the air to calm the rapids, but instead they calm other people by knocking them out. Keep the paddles down—they belong in the river. We use two kinds of strokes: forward and backward. Paddle on the right side to turn left and on the left side to turn right. You'll have to paddle to get through the rapids—hoping and wishing isn't good enough.

"Today you'll have a chance to get your raft stuck on a rock. You'll know when that happens because your friends will wave as they go floating past. Don't worry—they'll be hung up in five minutes too. Push on the rock with your paddles, and if you still don't move, you've done a splendid job. Don't sit there admiring your work, push harder, and if the raft *isn't* tilted up against a rock, move your body to the end of the raft that's *not* stuck, then try pushing again.

"If you fall out, and some of you will, tell the other people. Otherwise the splashing around that you'll do will sound just like all the rest of the river splashing around, and they might not miss you 'til later in the day. People in the raft should grab the person and pull him in. There's no graceful way—grab arms, legs, and (ahem) pants. Ladies, don't be offended—they'll be saving your life. While you're in the water, stay away from the front of the raft, and keep your feet high and pointed downstream, otherwise you might get a foot stuck in the river, which can be very dangerous.

"If your raft starts making funny 'hissing' noises, tell one of the guides. Okay, grab your raft and follow me, and don't let a car hit you when you cross the road."

With this ten-minute introduction, 60,000 people each year begin their trip down the Youghiogheny. Counting the legions of independent paddlers who don't go with an outfitter, there are over 100,000 rafters, kay-

Canoeing the Youghiogheny below Confluence
(paddling without life jacket is not recommended)

akers, and canoeists. This is the most floated whitewater in the United
States. Exciting rapids, spectacular scenery, clean water, adequate flow
throughout summer, and closeness to Pittsburgh are all conditions that
make the Yough popular.

Delaware or Lenni-Lenape Indians called the river "Yohoghany," meaning "stream flowing in a roundabout course." And it does. Beginning in
Maryland, the river is wild rapids until it's impounded by Youghiogheny
Dam, an Army Corps of Engineers' structure at the southern Pennsylvania
town of Confluence. Here the clean waters of Laurel Hill Creek and the
siltier, mine-acid drainage of the Casselman join the Yough. From Confluence to Ohiopyle, twelve miles of river are scenic and undeveloped, with
several Class II rapids that challenge beginning canoeists.

Swimming at Ohiopyle

Ohiopyle is the small remnant of a mountain town, the site of the river's best scenery and fullest recreational use. The Youghiogheny drops ninety feet in a boiling mile that includes hazardous rapids and the cataract of Ohiopyle Falls. Far more water flows over this falls than any other in Pennsylvania.

In 1754 George Washington's Indian guide wisely refused to lead a small army of colonists down the river, even though a loaded gun was said to be pointed at his head for encouragement. The French and Indian War skirmishes of Jumonville and Fort Necessity both took place nearby. Settlers arrived at Ohiopyle in the early 1800s, and from time to time they operated a saltworks, saw and pulp mill, spoke factory, shook (barrel parts) factory, and grist mill. The lumber and coal eras supported the most people, with the town's population peaking at about 700.

Old-time Ohiopyle was different from the place we see today. To hear what the river was like then, I looked up Shelby Mitchell, a "native" who grew up at the edge of the Yough fifty years ago.

"I've seen plenty of change since then. We swam in the river most every day, I guess, but that's about all it was used for. There weren't no fish, what with the tannery and acid from the mines, including our own Potter mine." He paused and reflected. "What we did up there ruined Cucumber Run. Then there was the industries that dumped their stuff in, and the sewage from Confluence. We used to cut ice and store it, y'know, and then people'd get diphtheria or typhoid when they drank the ice water. Nobody gave the river much thought; this rafting didn't start 'til about ten years ago.

"Oh, I s'pose the falls did make things a bit different around here. Us kids swam into it all the time, from the Ferncliff side, understand. God, you wouldn't want to go in from the side the mill was on. It was the strangers who'd come in and drown themselves, and then all the town'd go down there and watch for 'em to bring the body up."

I questioned why the town would be so entertained. "There just wasn't much else happenin', understand?"

"Who would look for the bodies?"

"Well, we all did, that is, me and my brother Udie, and old man Tharpe, and other guys in town. We pulled a lot of folks out, dead ones, that is. At night we'd drag hooks at the falls after someone drowned, and whenever the hook'd get stuck, one of us kids'd jump in and follow the hook down and pull it loose. If we couldn't find the body, we'd drop a charge into the water, and the blast'd sometimes bring 'em up. One fella didn't show up until he floated to Connellsville the next spring, but nine days seemed to be a normal time. That is, if we couldn't find 'em, they'd generally come up in nine days anyhow.

"That's all changed now. The park ranger won't let anybody swim at the falls. There's a hellish lot of people around, more, of course, than we'd ever seen. And there's more trouble, too, places broken into and such. Back then we'd have four or five drunks who'd fight with each other, but you knew who they were, and they didn't give anybody else trouble. I think the Kennedys got this raftin' stuff started, goin' down the Colorado and what not."

I asked about the state park and land that the Western Pennsylvania Conservancy bought in order to preserve the natural features of the area.

"The Conservancy I think has done a good thing in protectin' this land. Some folks get pretty upset about it all, but the way I see it is that Ohiopyle did its job—lumber, coal and the like, and now we've got recreation. But things go to extremes. Just how much land's the government need, anyway? Don't let anybody kid you, this social government's no good. Now there's even talk of buyin' land from Ohiopyle Park to Fort Necessity, about six miles on out the road, and that'd go right through this area."

The Ohiopyle Falls

"You don't really believe that, do you?" I knew this was not in the state's plans.

"Well, who knows? Guys'a been walkin' around here with maps and stuff, and nobody knows what'll happen. If they want to do something for the environment, why don't they stop this strip minin'?"

Bill and Adalene Holt also have spent their entire lives in Ohiopyle. Their families have lived in the area since the early 1800s. They ran the local store for forty years, and now they rent rooms in their antique-furnished guest house that sits with an older-era charm on a high bank overlooking the new park.

"We've had two waves of tourism in Ohiopyle," Bill began. "From 1900 to the thirties, and what you see here today. Things were pretty quiet in between times." That was how I remembered the town from visits I had made ten and twenty years ago. "At about 1900, excursion trains began bringing passengers, two trains from Pittsburgh and one from Cumberland. People'd come up and back the same day, or they'd sell their return trip ticket for fifty cents and then stay overnight."

"The ladies wore long ruffled dresses, and they carried parasols," Adalene added. "Local folks would board visitors, meeting them with fringe-covered surreys at the train station. The three hotels would be filled, and at the Ferncliff they'd have outdoor dining and dancing with good orchestras. Bill's uncle ran the Ferncliff."

"What happened to the hotels and the people?" There are no hotels today.

"You're looking at it right there," Bill answered before I finished asking. He waved a hand toward the cars along Main Street. "The automobile put an end to the railroad's profits, and they quit running excursion trains."

"It's different now, isn't it?"

Adalene and a few visiting neighbor ladies agreed. The way they shook their heads, it was clear they liked it a lot more the way it used to be. "How did all this get started?" I asked, as we looked down at the park, at four boys carrying a rubber raft, a mother with her children coming out of the store, and a young girl wearing a T-shirt lettered "JanSport"—one of the backpacking equipment manufacturers.

"Lance Martin was the first outfitter," Bill began. "For his first year, he took fifty people all summer, using one raft that he blew up with my Electrolux sweeper. He'd sleep overnight in the garage, back over at the old house. That was about 1965."

"As the town changed and the park was developed, what affected local people the most?"

"Well, the *land*," Adalene said, wondering why I didn't have a better grasp of the obvious. "Twenty-nine houses on Main Street were taken."

"Most of the people didn't want to sell," Bill added. "Many were old, with nothing much to live for after their places were gone." I wanted to talk to some of these people. "They're mostly all dead now," Bill explained, "and a lot of the younger people weren't here to really know what it was like. Some people got $3,000, which might have been the value of their building, but how could those folks ever buy a new house for that price?"

"Why did they have to do it *that* way?" Adalene asked, as if I would know. "The town could have been fixed up nice, with shops and places for people to go."

"And if they'd left the picnic area at Ferncliff Park, across the river, they wouldn't have needed all that land in Ohiopyle," one of the neighbor ladies added. "Oh, the picnics and ball games we used to have over there!"

I tried to answer. "I think that a lot of government agencies are taking a softer approach now, without buying up so many homes, and relocation assistance is now better, but none of that helps you people."

I changed the subject. "What do folks think of the park now—does all the activity bother you?" I was thinking of the 800,000 visitors, the parking lots, and the vast cultural gulf between the people of Ohiopyle and the melange of whitewater enthusiasts, urbanites, and other people who storm through town.

"Not so much anymore," one of the neighbor women said, "but there used to be all kinds of riff-raff down there." She pointed at the park again. "People would even swim—well, nude."

"There's really not much of any problem now," Bill said. "Of course, some people'd complain if you mowed their grass for them, but by and large, visitors stay down there and we stay up here."

Cucumber Rapid of the Youghiogheny, below Ohiopyle

Cucumber Falls, a tributary to the Youghiogheny

Rafters in Cucumber Rapid below Ohiopyle

I wanted to hear more about the Youghiogheny and the state park, so I drove out the old Dinner-Bell Road to Meadow Run bridge where the state park headquarters is now located. The receptionist was friendly and asked me to be seated. A few minutes later, Larry Adams, the superintendent, said I could step in his office.

"What can I do for you?" he asked.

I was a little surprised at how young he looked, with a cool but helpful, honest air about him. We began talking about the river, the park, and whitewater rafting.

"Actually, rafting and kayaking amount to only 10 percent of our use," Larry said. "About 800,000 people come here during the year, and most of them just look around, maybe have a picnic."

"Do you have problems with overuse?"

"Crowds are heavy only on major holidays. Overuse or crowding is not a limiting factor, generally."

I could see that I was going to get answers, but the superintendent wasn't the rambling type and I'd have to ask a lot of questions. "Permits and quotas are now established and enforced for commercial outfitters. Do you see a permit requirement coming for private individual boaters as well?"

"No, but it's hard to tell for sure."

"Do you find many people disappointed when they meet crowds of other floaters on the river?"

"Sometimes the kayakers and canoeists find that a problem. It doesn't seem to bother the rafters. Most rafters, of course, are less experienced. Most people who come seem to be really pleased. They like the park."

"What special kinds of problems do you face here that you didn't have in the other parks where you've worked?"

Pause. "This is a unique park. Safety is the biggest thing, the biggest issue. We've cut down on the number of drownings—no swimming is allowed at the falls, no inner tubes in the rapids. Life jackets are required, and rafting is closed when water level is over three feet at the launch site."

The outfitters on the Yough were up for relicensing in 1977, and it looked as if it could become a hot subject. Under past "temporary" agreements, only four companies were allowed on the river, taking a maximum of eighty people per trip and two trips per day. The Commonwealth assumed authority to regulate the operations, since the access area is within park boundaries. The rafting companies limited their numbers, with the state providing assurance that no new competition would be allowed in. "It's difficult to regulate commercial operators," was about all the superintendent would say.

"How do you identify outfitters who bring their people and equipment in for one day? They could look like a church group or the YMCA."

"They do, and sometimes we don't."

"What's the state's position on the proposed national scenic-river designation?" I asked.

"The state's not for it," he answered. "We'd rather administer our own program. All the federal government would do is add an extra level of administration."

"What complaint do you hear most often, and what do you think could be the biggest problem in the park?"

He thought for a few seconds and fidgeted with his cigarette. "Ferncliff Park. The old picnic area and ballfield was closed after the area was designated a National Natural Landmark. It's a unique area, biologically speaking, and the park was not consistent with landmark status. Some people were used to going there for picnics and other activity, and now they can't do that. Things are going pretty well now, but new coal mining that could pollute the river is always a threat."

Cindy and I left our camp site early for a sunrise photo of the Youghiogheny, then we went to the store for a cup of coffee. While substantial block letters at the top of the building still say "Holt's Department Store," it's obvious that a switch has been made over the last five or ten years. The snack bar is now located where a good selection of clothing and hardware had been. Bill Holt even carried appliances for the townspeople and mountaineers, but now there were pinball machines: "Wildlife, A Game of Skill," with a picture of an apeman and a full-bosomed female wearing a small fraction of a leopard's skin. An older fellow who worked in a nearby strip mine sat across from us, and we talked a little, mainly about fishing in the Yough, which has improved incredibly over the past few years. The waitress came out. Without speaking, she poured a cup of coffee for the man and didn't quite seem to notice us.

"Ja hear about the drownin'?" she asked but didn't wait for an answer. "I just knew it'd happen; there hasn't been one *all* year." Details of the report had stuck in her mind. "They say her life jacket was ripped right off, and it took a half-hour to pull her out. There's *no way* I'm goin' down that river!"

Cass Chestnut is a river guide. Running whitewater is his livelihood. It's hard to be a good guide—an expert's skills in paddling are needed, along with a thorough knowledge of safety, equipment, and the river. A flair for entertaining is essential. In spite of cold weather, soaking clothes, and a few folks who are scared out of their shivering skins, the guide has to keep the clients happy, or at least try. Cass's head is full of river experience that comes out unwinnowed, unstrained.

"It was a real bummer. I had three months to go before the Peace Corps, and so I figured, 'Cass, you really enjoyed that trip down the Yough—why not get a job for a few months?' So I wrote to this outfitter, and he said, 'Sure, come on down.' You guessed it, I've been here ever since. Back in

Rowing a raft on the Youghiogheny below Ohiopyle

those days, if you wanted to be a river guide, you lived a river guide's life—what I mean is, you got $300 a year, and you hoped it came by December. Nowadays, if you want to be a river guide, you have to live a river guide's life, if you know what I mean." He motioned to his old silver trailer, provided free to the guide staff. "The place is—well, I spend most of my time outside anyway. Say, can I get you a cup of tea?"

Cass came out of the trailer armed with a hot cup of red zinger and a bag of oatmeal cookies, flipping a thumb toward a rusty metal bed that sat under a maple tree. "Lately I've even been sleeping out here. I quit drinking altogether. I feel great. I quit smoking except for special occasions, and this is a special occasion. Want a buzz?"

I didn't want to smoke. "No, thanks."

"Where was I? Oh yeah, I could write a book about the river—'The Death of the Yough,' how's that sound? You get tired of some of these guys, the macho types, know what I mean? A few years ago it was different, for sure. People came 'cause they wanted to see the river and have fun. They looked at the trees. Now it's the thing to do; they heard about it at a party. 'Well, *I* rafted the Yough.' You know, some of the girls around are really good in their kayaks, and these goons'd meet 'em in town and brag about how they were going down the river, trying to make an impression or something. The 'quasi wilderness experience' gets a little more 'quasi' all the time. Some days I'd just rather patch rafts. But people make it interesting, too. Once in a while I leave the kayak in the garage and go in a raft to be with some other folks."

"Isn't that slow and not much fun?" I asked, but there's more to running a river than whitewater.

"You should have seen the young lady in that raft! Really, the people are okay so long as they're not bummin' off the rest of the trip. They gotta keep their water splashing battles to themselves, in other words.

"People come from all over—Cleveland, Baltimore, especially Pittsburgh, and some even from Chicago. Once we had this double group—a gang of gay weightlifters along with a bunch of deaf-mutes. The weightlifters would do their gestures, you know? and the deaf-mutes rattled off their sign language. Then there's our guides standing on the rocks waving which way to go—" and he did a quick imitation of half a dozen arm motions that were commonly seen on that day. "Then once in a while something really neat happens, like this picture. Hold on." Cass disappeared again into the trailer and emerged holding a snapshot. "I met this dude on the Slippery Rock—now there's a good stream. You seen it?"

"Yeah."

"Anyway, this guy took my picture doing an ender. A few weeks ago he showed up with it as a gift. I don't know how he even found out I was here. The only neater thing was the lady who claimed to be my wife in a former lifetime."

We talked for a while about the outfitters' operations and the way guides handle safety. "At first when they started talking about sixty or eighty people per trip, the guides said, 'My God, no, what will we do with them?' But it worked out okay, I guess, with more guides on the river, Each outfitter is allowed to take eighty people per trip, see, in order to not overrun the river. You know how they came up with that number? That's what two shuttle busses hold. The outfitters' contracts are up this year. I mean, a new contract has to be made. Everybody's kind of anxious and waitin' to see what'll happen."

He went on. "You know none of the outfitters has ever had a drowning on the Yough?"

"That's kind of amazing, isn't it?" I said.

"Don't get me wrong; we have had some people die on us. Two heart

Double Hydraulic Rapid, Youghiogheny River

Kayakers in Cucumber Rapid

attacks, both at the bottom of Swimmer's Rapids. You know Swimmer's don't you?"

"Sure."

"The first was on the day the Goodyear blimp was over the river. Yeah, we came around a bend, and there it was. We got to Swimmer's, and the guy just kind of slumped over in his rubber kayak. We pulled him in and gave him mouth-to-mouth resuscitation. His lunch kept comin' up, and I think it was a month, no, probably two, before I had any peanut butter sandwiches again. A doctor was on the trip and pronounced him dead after forty minutes or so.

"The guides've saved a lot of other people too—independent, private boaters, I mean. Like the duffers who rent a raft from this guy in town. It's gotten so we just can't babysit everybody. We've quit throwing his people ropes. . . . That's his job.

"We keep backboards hid at six places along the route, in case we ever get a broken back or something like that. We now use type five jackets— the safest kind—it's the law for inflatable boats." At last Cass stopped talking for a second.

"When we went down with you," I said, "there were people who really didn't belong out there. They weren't in very good shape, and some of the older women looked terrified. What do you do when someone just doesn't want to go any farther?"

"They mostly just last it out. Once a girl fell out at Cucumber and didn't want back in, so I got in her raft and kind of calmed her down for a while." Cass winked at me but really at the memory. "That was an exciting day; half the rafts were flipping at Dimple Rock.

"That's where the California girl drowned yesterday. They had a big rowing rig, seventeen feet or so. Great on western rivers, but here it's a little too tight." I had just rowed my twelve-foot Avon raft down the river, and Cass was right—there are a lot of rocks to maneuver around, and oars require a little more width of river than paddles. Worse problems, however, came from other rafts that would get too close, immobilizing the oars.

"Is the number of boaters increasing?"

"Oh, sure. Commercial use, I think, will level off, but independent boaters just keep coming and coming. There'll probably be a permit re-quirement for them in a few years. Some days the river's too crowded—seventeen or eighteen hundred people might go down on a weekend. People ought to come during the week. You know, those folks are differ-ent, too—the ones on Monday through Friday seem to see more, to enjoy it more. They're more interested."

He paused for a second, but it was never much more than that. "One of the neatest things is just being here. You know, it's a good place to *be*. I've thought of building a cabin. The people are great; we really get along well. They accept the guides, like the lady who runs the post office. No prob-lems like you might run into other places. Some of the local young people are now paddling too. There are some really good local paddlers, for sure."

I always figured a river runner would take to running rivers everywhere. "Have you thought of guiding in the West, on wild rivers out there?"

Cass thought a little longer than his usual split second. "No, it pays pretty good here, $45 or $50 a day for a good experienced guide. But I'm thinking of moving on. I've got an application for Hershey Medical Center for medical assistant training, you know, do a lot of doctor-type jobs in rural areas. Being a guide all your life would be a little tough, for sure. Jumpin' into a wet suit to paddle a freezin' river when you're forty or fifty years old? I figure we each ought to be the best person we can, and so some day I'll be movin' on, to do something better. For people, I mean. That's what I like about guiding. Wilderness belongs to everybody, and this is a way to get them there. If you enjoy it, it can do something *to* you—it's expansive. People who enjoy it might even want to save it. They'll know it better. They'll know it's worth something."

The Youghiogheny below Railroad Rapid

Tionesta Creek below Sheffield

Ohio Basin River Sketches

Tionesta Creek

Tionesta Creek is probably best known for its scout camp where many thousands of western Pennsylvania boys have gone for weekends and week-long summer camping sessions. Most of the watershed is in Allegheny National Forest, including an outstanding tract of virgin timber at Hearts Content, a smaller stand at Tionesta Scenic Area, and a recreational site and wilderness valley at Minister Creek.

Below the small town of Sheffield, Tionesta and its South Branch join and follow a south and westerly course to the backwaters of Tionesta Dam, where the Boy Scout camp is located. The creek meets the Allegheny only a few miles below the impoundment. Fishing is good, attracting many anglers from western Pennsylvania and eastern Ohio. There are no major rapids, and the stream makes an excellent canoe trip in early spring. The confluence of Tionesta and the South Branch is an interesting and scenic lowland area, and massive hemlocks can be seen above the eastern bank, a half mile downstream.

Oil Creek

The oil industry began along this stream of northwestern Pennsylvania. Drake's Well, the first to be drilled, is located on the creek's east bank near Titusville. Evidence of old drilling is seen everywhere—well casing, rusting pipes, and abandoned machinery. Active wells continue, and refineries are crowded in the highly industrialized lower creek, which meets the Allegheny at Oil City. In this part of the state chloride pollution is extensive, resulting from oil and gas recovery operations and from natural upwelling of deep brines.

A state park has been established along the stream from Titusville to Petroleum Center, a distance of about eighteen miles. Both sides of Oil Creek are included, and a bicycle trail is being built through the park's entire length. While the area has been repeatedly logged, drilled, and farmed in past years, development has not occurred in this reach. Canoeing can be done in springtime, and fishing is possible above the industrialized areas.

French Creek below Utica

French Creek

Flowing southward through farmlands that are only twenty miles from Lake Erie beaches, French Creek is one of the largest Allegheny tributaries. The stream's origins are in New York; then its waters drift in a great arc to Meadville and southeastward to the town of Franklin. During the geologic past, prior to the Wisconsin Ice Age, the Allegheny River flowed north toward Lake Erie through the approximate channel of today's French Creek. The direction of flow was reversed when continental ice masses blocked the water's northern escape.

Uplands and headwaters of French Creek are sometimes swampy or marshy, serving as an excellent waterfowl habitat. Most of the stream is slow, winding through pastoral farmlands, but the lower reaches are more confined and enclosed by wooded hillsides. A pleasant and easy canoe trip can be run in the springtime from Meadville, and the creek is popular for warm-water fishing. Another French Creek, near Philadelphia, is a small stream being considered for the state scenic rivers system.

The Conemaugh and Flood City

The Conemaugh is a major stream of western Pennsylvania, where its waters form the Kiskiminetas, then join the Allegheny. Mine acid, Bethlehem Steel, and raw sewage devastated the Conemaugh and Kiski years ago, in a pattern that continues. The river causes fish kills in the Allegheny.

High water was inevitable at Johnstown, on the low terrace between Stony Creek and the Little Conemaugh. Mountainsides flushed their rains to this urban meeting place; flooding occurred fifteen times between 1808 and 1888. May of 1889, however, was a different case. Heavy rains filled South Fork Lake. At the time it was the world's largest earthen dam, seventy feet high, originally built for the state canal system. Pittsburgh industrialists bought the lake and settled at their comfortable summer retreats, but only after repairing a breach. They filled it with dirt, rubble, and cow manure, leaving a low spot in the center and partially filling the spillway to block in the fish. On May 31 waters flowed over the repaired dam. The rubble loosened, then burst. A forty-foot wave reached town without warning one hour later. Twenty-two hundred people drowned or burned in a fiery mass that congealed above the great stone railroad bridge. It's the same bridge you see today, just below the point where the two rivers meet.

People rebuilt, of course, to be flooded again in 1936, when water levels surpassed all records. After this the Army Corps of Engineers played an important role, channeling the rivers in concrete walls, and concluding, "We believe the flood troubles of the city are at an end."

Boosterism caught hold for "flood-free Johnstown," and this was largely true until July 19, 1977. Nearly twelve inches of rain fell in seven hours. It was a freak storm, like others that occur once or twice every year, somewhere in the country. The 1936 record was surpassed, and five small earthen dams failed. Laurel Run sent fifteen feet of water through the flood-plain neighborhoods. Eighty-seven people were killed. Incredibly, communities had decided that flood insurance and zoning were not necessary.

So much for a false sense of security.

What's happening now? A ride up the Johnstown incline can show you the birds-eye view. There's rebuilding, but there are plenty of vacant lots, too. A developer proposes an elevated shopping mall near the confluence. Bethlehem Steel, its tracks and buildings and furnaces winding beyond the horizon along the Little Conemaugh, threatened a shutdown after the flood, but is hanging on with an Environmental Protection Agency extension for pollution abatement. Faced with unnecessary hardship and cost, people's willingness to stay and rebuild is being shaken.

Of 2,800 communities in Pennsylvania, 2,468 are partially in the flood plain. Statewide, $7 billion worth of property has been lost to floods through the years. In spite of $3 billion which has been spent on flood-control works, damages continue to grow. Local government fails to prevent new building on lowlands, while logging, urbanization, and some modern farming techniques vastly increase the magnitude of storm-water problems.

Along with the Hurricane Agnes flood of 1972, the submerged dikes of Wilkes-Barre and the inadequacies of the flood-insurance program, Johnstown points to the need for an effective, obligatory flood-plain management program. Senator Franklin Kury has championed the issue since Agnes waters subsided, but local government and developers staunchly kept the legislature from action. In 1978 a Pennsylvania flood-plain management law passed, but in a weakened form.

Little Conemaugh at Johnstown

The Conemaugh also includes a gorge 1,350 feet deep. Above Johnstown is Stony Creek (not to be confused with Stony Creek north of Harrisburg). Though pollution is severe in this stream, whose waters range from coal black to bright orange, the valley is undeveloped and scenic in some places. A formidable gorge forms north of U.S. Route 30.

Loyalhanna Creek joins the Kiskiminetas near Saltsburg. Beginning on Laurel Hill near Linn Run and Laurel Mountain state parks, water of Loyalhanna is better than that of other tributaries, since coal mining has been less extensive and many acres are publicly owned.

Slippery Rock Creek

Like the Youghiogheny of southwestern Pennsylvania or Pine Creek in the north central highlands, Slippery Rock Creek is an outstanding stream of its region. In the northwestern portion of the state, no other waterway has the scenic appeal of moss-covered boulders, churning whitewater, and deep green pools that are found in the gorge below Route 422. At the end of the Wisconsin Ice Age, the gorge was formed when a terminal moraine holding a massive meltwater lake eroded, releasing waters in a torrent and carving the rocky passage that the creek now follows. Recognizing the need to preserve the scenic, geological, and historic landmark, the Western Pennsylvania Conservancy acquired 2,000 acres along the Slippery Rock, including an abandoned grist mill. Later the Conservancy resold the land to the Commonwealth, and McConnell's Mill State Park was established. The restored mill is now open for public touring, and scenic trails can be hiked upstream and down. A maze of boulders and rocky cliffs are found on the western side of the creek, where crevasses and tunnels can be explored and climbed, with adequate safety precautions.

The Slippery Rock's plunge through the gorge involves highly "technical" rapids. The stream is not large, and expert maneuvering around many rocks and obstacles is essential if the kayaker or canoeist is to stay afloat. Good trout fishing is also returning to the Slippery Rock after years of acid pollution.

Headwaters include Muddy Creek, where 3,200-acre Lake Arthur was built in the late 1960s near the site of the ancient meltwater lake. Moraine State Park, another Conservancy project, surrounds the new impoundment and draws large crowds of Pittsburghers and other western Pennsylvanians on summer weekends. National Boy Scout jamborees have been held here several times. To improve water quality, the state engaged in costly mine reclamation programs. Additional stripping remains a threat. After heated debates, a new mine was opened along the boundary of McConnell's Mill Park.

Slippery Rock Creek below McConnell's Mill

Above the Beaver River, the Slippery Rock meets Connoquenessing
Creek. This stream is a popular warm-water fishery where bluegills, bass,
and sunfish thrive. While most of the Connoquenessing meanders through
farmland, the creek forms a formidable set of Class III rapids in its lower
reaches.

Beaver River

Much of the land in northwestern Pennsylvania drains toward the Beaver
River, which begins at New Castle with the confluence of the Mahoning
and Shenango. Over 3,000 square miles are in this system, the Mahoning
and Shenango River basins draining about 1,000 square miles each. Char-
acteristically, rivers of industrialized western Pennsylvania are sluggish and
foul, with a few exceptions. The Shenango begins in Pymatuning Lake and
marsh areas of the north, incomparable for their populations of migrating
water birds. Coming from Ohio, the Mahoning is exceptional too in
another way—noted as one of the dirtiest, most fetid of American waterways, regarded as a sewer more than a river. In 1977, the state of Pennsylvania and the Sierra Club won a lawsuit against the federal Environmental
Protection Agency. The U.S. Court of Appeals' decision disallowed EPA's

unprecedented water quality control exemptions to eight Mahoning steel mills.

The Beaver River is slow moving, impounded, and highly developed. Though the water can be unhealthy to swimmers, the lower river provides recreation; boating activity has exploded over the past fifteen years. Motorboats were uncommon when I grew up along the Beaver and Ohio rivers in the fifties and early sixties. A high school friend had a boat that we cruised in, daring each other to jump in the foul broth. Now the water is a little better and packed with expensive fleets. An annual regatta near the mouth of the Beaver draws thousands of people each summer.

Casselman River

The Casselman rises near Grantsville, in the state of Maryland, and flows counterclockwise in a large arc around Mt. Davis to Confluence, Pennsylvania, where it meets the great Youghiogheny. Through much of its course the Casselman is a rugged and wild river, but acid mine drainage has nearly decimated aquatic life and has stained an orange riverbed.

Mine drainage does not eliminate the thrills and challenge of a whitewater canoeing experience, and several reaches from Garrett to Confluence are favorites of canoe and kayak travelers when water is at medium and high levels. Boulders are plentiful, forming powerful chutes of water and pockets of bubbling eddies where boaters can stop to rest and plan their next moves through the current. Visitors should not park vehicles or use private land for access without asking permission from landowners, as problems regarding trespassing have occurred. Rapids are rated Class II and III, a good choice for experienced paddlers who might travel to Ohiopyle and find the Youghiogheny too high to comfortably run.

Much has been done to reclaim areas of strip mining and to improve water quality. Better fishing on the Youghiogheny is evidence of this, but the Casselman still has a long way to go.

Wills Creek

The Potomac tends to be a forgotten river system in Pennsylvania, though its tributaries include a total of 1,582 square miles in the south central mountains. Waters of the Allegheny ridges flow southward to feed the "National River," as it was called by President Lyndon Johnson. At one point, the Potomac's north shore is only a few miles from the Pennsylvania state border.

Major tributaries include Conococheague Creek, largest in length and in letters, Monocacy Creek, which runs through Gettysburg, Tonoloway Creek, Evitts Creek, and Wills Creek.

Wills is the wildest and most rugged of the group. It cuts a stony gorge eastward through the mountains before joining broader and southward-tending valleys that are typical of the region. The basin begins east of Myersdale, where two remote forks switch back through an erratic topography, then plunge together from Fairhope to Hyndman, where the stream bends southward to the city of Cumberland. Dark and rounded boulders characterize much of the upper stream bed. Trout fishing is generally good. Kayaking and whitewater canoeing in covered or decked boats is possible during very high runoff, but the creek is extremely difficult and only for experts.

Laurel Hill Creek

While many of the waterways of western Pennsylvania have been developed, mined, and polluted, Laurel Hill Creek has retained many qualities of the natural river. The stream has been "saved," in effect, by Laurel Mountain, a long backbone of the Appalachians that angles northeastward from the Ohiopyle area to Johnstown. This is the second in a rugged set of paralleling ridges, and as such, headlong development of the greater Pittsburgh area comes to an abrupt stop on mountain flanks to the west.

Recognizing the beauty of the land and its recreational value to the metropolitan area, the Commonwealth has acquired many acres on the mountain. Kooser and Laurel Hill state parks form the headwaters of Laurel Hill Creek, while state forest and game lands cover western portions of the basin. Dairy farms blend with forested passages of the stream, and trout fishing is excellent. Just below Route 653, west of New Lexington, is a Burr Truss-type covered bridge, built in the 1800s. With high water, canoe runs on Laurel Hill Creek are a challenging Class III.

In 1975 the "Laurel Hill Study" was prepared by University of Pennsylvania graduate students, under the sponsorship of the Western Pennsylvania Conservancy. Important environmental features of the region were identified and evaluated, leading to recommendations for overall protection and use. To implement the study, the Laurel Highlands Conservation and Development Project was formed with William Curry as its director. It is hoped that this type of long-range view, with combined action of private and public interests, will be successful in preserving Laurel Hill and its creek.

The Monongahela River

The Monongahela is one of the six largest waterways in Pennsylvania. Most people know the river as a flatwater industrial pool at Homestead, McKeesport, and Pittsburgh, where riverboat cruises can be taken through the Three Rivers urban area. The basin encompasses over 7,000 square miles, though much of this is in West Virginia, where the Cheat River, a tributary, incorporates a wild-water canyon and outstanding streams for the paddler and naturalist. Some of these are the forks named Shavers, Glady, Laurel, and Dry. Red Creek drains the Dolly Sods wild area. Otter Creek is another wilderness area, and the Blackwater is famous for its falls.

The "Mon" forms at the West Fork and Tygart rivers near Fairmont, West Virginia, and runs 128 miles to the Allegheny at Pittsburgh. All of this is navigable to motorized, commercial craft.

Like other big rivers, the "Mon" has a share of the nation's history. George Washington explored its upper reaches, looking for a colonial northwest passage—a waterway from the Potomac to the Ohio. Local folks advised the Virginian that the Cheat was navigable. Luckily for the nation, George didn't try it. That style of river running has been better left to Kennedy on the Colorado and Carter on the Middle Fork of the Salmon.

One of the first flatboats was built and launched from Brownsville in 1782. Jacob Yoder spent two months drifting 2,000 miles to the lower Mississippi. Commercial shipping came early: the Monongahela Navigation Company was formed in 1808 to build dams but the company failed before its impounds were constructed. A second company formed in 1836 and had six locks and dams in place by 1844. Similar developments on the lower Youghiogheny, a major tributary, washed out in 1854 and were not rebuilt.

The Navigation Company did well until the government interfered in 1886, when Congress stipulated that no tolls could be charged for shipping that originated above government dams in West Virginia. So began the pork-barrel/special interest lobby of river navigation, whereby shippers run for free with the government doing the work. The political and economic forces generated in this way have drag-lined themselves up many a stream, dredging, channeling, and damming the big arteries of riverine America. Ongoing controversy about the Tennessee-Tombigbee waterway of Alabama and Lock and Dam 26 on the Mississippi are one of the results. The government bought the Monongahela Navigation Company in 1897 after a year of condemnation proceedings.

As a centerpiece of intensive use and abuse, the Monongahela may be unsurpassed. One hundred sixty miles of tributary streams are acidic with coal-mine waste. Sewage and industrial pollution are rampant, and thermal discharges overheat the water at power plant and industrial sites. Burrell and Davidson's guidebook to West Virginia rivers calls the "Mon" the sewer of northern West Virginia. Yet it has improved. Powerboating is popular through the length of the river, with access and marinas at Millsboro, Rice's

Monongahela at Pittsburgh

Landing, Point Marion, and other sites. Some communities show a renewed interest in their riverfront, with open space and park developments.

Appropriation of water is burgeoning as a major issue on this southwestern river. Steel mills, seventeen public water suppliers, and three power plants have a deep and lasting thirst. Much of the flow in drought periods comes from Tygart Reservoir in West Virginia, which was built to augment navigation flow. The federal government has control of these waters and may prohibit any diversion that would interfere with the quantity needed for commercial barge traffic. The state of Pennsylvania recommends another reservoir in West Virginia—Rowlesburg Dam on the Cheat. The target reach, from Rowlesburg to Parsons, is an easy rolling river, scenic

Monongahela at Pittsburgh

with farmland, bluffs, and a healthy family of bass. West Virginia opposes the dam, arguing successfully to the Ohio River Basin Commission, which dropped the site from its Level B study. Pennsylvania holds fast, as with the Tocks Island Dam proposal on the Delaware, identifying some extreme options for times of drought: a moratorium on growth, relocation of major water users, importation of water, and temporary abandonment of commercial navigation. Consumptive use of water—using it and not returning it to the stream—is on a sharp increase through much of Pennsylvania, due largely to electric power-plant cooling, especially nuclear plants. The question looms greater and greater, here and on other Pennsylvania rivers: who will get the water when it starts to run short?

Ohio River, with Pittsburgh and the confluence of the Allegheny (left)
and Monogahela (right) in background

The Ohio River

The Ohio's volume of water is second only to the Susquehanna's among Pennsylvania streams. This becomes one of the largest American rivers; it carries twice the volume of the Mississippi where they join in Cairo, Illinois. It is a historical river—Fort Duquesne, a French frontier outpost, was strategically located at the Ohio's origin, where the Allegheny and Monongahela join. The site was one of highest importance, marking the gateway to interior American travel as well as routes north and southeast. The French and English fought repeatedly over this location during the French and Indian War. Upon English capture, Duquesne was renamed Fort Pitt; hence the frontier town was called "Pittsburgh." With nearby coalfields, rail lines, and commercial navigation throughout the Ohio's length, the city eventually became the industrial giant of the nation.

Flatboats carried many western settlers from busy Pittsburgh wharves to the Mississippi, where they boarded steamboats for St. Louis and routes west. Luxurious stern-wheeler riverboats churned up and down the Ohio through the nineteenth century. To facilitate river commerce, a continuous series of nineteen locks and dams was completed in 1929. The 981-mile river carries more cargo than the Panama Canal, and 29 million people now live in the fourteen-state basin. The Port of Pittsburgh is the largest inland waterway port of the United States.

Today the "Golden Triangle" marks the Ohio's source, where tall buildings show Pittsburgh's successful efforts to reclaim and reuse an area of abandoned structures and warehouses. Point State Park includes an interesting reconstruction of Fort Duquesne, though it is surrounded by freeways that may pose hazards greater than French guards. Downriver, development of heavy industry is nearly continuous—Jones and Laughlin steel mills at Aliquippa envelop miles of water frontage, and the Conway railroad yards, once the largest in the world, are still heavily used.

Most natural values of the river have been utterly destroyed. Industry, railroads, and highways allow only a weedy growth of vegetation to meet the water's edge, and pollution is severe. Manufacturing wastes include toxic materials: cyanide, phenolics, PCB's, and other effluent; however, water quality has improved over the past era, which was marked by total indifference to the environment.

Allegheny County has 20,023 registered motorboats, more than the next three Pennsylvania counties combined. The Three Rivers Regatta attracts several hundred thousand people. Downriver, motorboating and water skiing are also popular in places like the big southward bend where the towns of Beaver, Rochester, and Monaca border the river.

From a distance the Ohio remains an impressive sight. The three rivers—Allegheny, Monongahela, and Ohio—can be seen from overlooks on Mt. Washington, south of downtown Pittsburgh. In the town of Beaver, River Road follows the rim of a high terrace, with attractive houses on one side

Ohio River at Beaver

and scenic river views on the other. Sandstone cliffs rise from the southern shore, and riverboats push their barges of freight. At Georgetown, a small settlement near the state border, one can see an old river village and an uncommonly natural view of the wide Ohio waters.

The Delaware Basin

High on the Lehigh

In northeastern Pennsylvania, the Pocono Mountains have been a popular recreation area for nearly 100 years. Brown boggy waters signify land that used to be a maze of glacial lakes, now bordered by Scranton and Wilkes-Barre's urban fringe. New York City and Philadelphia are not far away, and so the trade in lodges, golf courses, car racing, skiing, motorboating, and honeymooning has been a vigorous one, overshadowing but certainly not eliminating the more traditional fishing and hunting. The lakes of Tobyhanna, Bear, Bradys, Arrowhead, and Pocono lie at high headwaters; together with hundreds of swamps and wetlands, they join to form the Lehigh River.

One can accurately picture the Lehigh in three distinct sections, the first being headwaters and a small but turbulent river, growing with amber swampwater and cutting an ever deeper valley into the glaciated plateau. Notable tributaries are the rapid Bear Creek and the famous trout stream, Tobyhanna.

At Francis E. Walters Dam, the continuum of river is broken with a mile-long pool that extends far upstream when flood gates are shut. Below the reservoir begins the wild course of the Lehigh River Gorge, where the stream drops 735 feet in thirty-three miles. The first seven miles offer excellent Class II and III whitewater, though the topography of the gorge has not yet fully evolved and shorelines are sometimes developed with roads, railroads, and homes. Below Lehigh Tannery, the gorge begins in earnest, and whitewater continues to mount in a crescendo, reaching its exciting peak at Mile-Long Rapids above the town of Jim Thorpe. Scenery becomes spectacular, with jagged outcrops on ridge-lines that rise 1,000 feet. In Pennsylvania only the canyons of Pine Creek and the upper West Branch of the Susquehanna compare, although the Lehigh is many times more turbulent than either.

Much of this ends at Jim Thorpe, where the Lehigh becomes a river of man, with highways, railroads, switchyards, industry, and commerce crowding its banks. The lower river penetrates the industrial metropolis of Allentown-Bethlehem.

Of the three sections, the gorge is clearly the highlight. If you are look-

Opposite: Rock climbing above the Lehigh, lower gorge

ing for wild whitewater, here is the place to go. Next to the Youghiogheny of southwestern Pennsylvania, this Pocono river is the roughest big stream in the state. For years it has been a mecca to whitewater enthusiasts.

Protection efforts in the Lehigh Gorge began with the Game Commission's acquisition of much acreage on the east shore. The Penn Haven Rod and Gun Club retains control of twelve miles on the west side, an area members zealously guard with firearms, preventing boaters and other strangers from setting foot on it.

In 1970 the statewide planning report titled "Outdoor Recreation Horizons" recommended that the Department of Forests and Waters (now the Department of Environmental Resources) acquire most lands in the gorge for a state park. "This area should be preserved in its present condition," the report added, "with development primarily limited to construction of scenic hiking trails and primitive camping areas." The Horizons report recognized the Pocono region of the Commonwealth as one of the major recreation areas of northeastern United States, but identified the gorge as a place that "should be left relatively undeveloped." Plans proceeded for establishment of a Lehigh Gorge State Park, but acquisition of property became entangled, and interminable delays set in. Instead of the Department of Environmental Resources, where Secretary Goddard would have acted with dispatch, the Department of General Services was given money to buy lands, assuring a snail's pace to protection while property values soar. Some owners will reap windfalls at public expense. It was not the park but another state program that was to bring renewed and concentrated attention to the middle Lehigh.

In December of 1972 Governor Shapp signed into law a Pennsylvania Scenic Rivers Act, which established a framework to designate streams for special protection and management. Efforts had begun several years earlier when, in the wake of the National Wild and Scenic Rivers Act, a number of states began to enact their own programs. Conservationists from State College and Williamsport collected samples of bills and forwarded them to Representative (now Senator) Franklin Kury, who began the long and tedious process of lawmaking.

The bill was supported by environmentalists, though some were skeptical. "The Pennsylvania law will allow for appeasement of conservation interests while providing a means of river protection that is less secure than national designation," some people said. "It will be used as a reason to oppose the federal program." In support of the bill they added, "Nationally significant streams can be included in the national system, but we have scores of rivers that deserve protection, though they are only of statewide significance. They are the ones that should be in the state system."

Legislators carefully avoided questions of which river in which system. The act simply stated that "the Department of Environmental Resources shall study, conduct public hearings . . . and from time to time submit to the Governor and to the General Assembly proposals for the designation of rivers or sections of rivers as components of the Pennsylvania Scenic River System." In a very important but often overlooked paragraph, the law refers to the national system: "The Secretary of Environmental Resources is directed to encourage and assist any federal studies for inclusion of Pennsylvania rivers in a national scenic rivers system."

A task force was formed to assist the Department in completing recommendations for waterways that should be studied under the new law. Two hundred forty-five streams were identified, and sixty-one were recommended as highest priority. The Secretary of the Department chose three of these for study in 1976—Pine Creek, the Schuylkill River, and the Lehigh Gorge.

Kayakers, Lehigh at Mile-Long Rapids

The intent of the Scenic Rivers Act is clear: "to protect these values and to practice sound conservation policies and practices within this Scenic Rivers System." Details, however, are largely absent from the law. While a stream must be free of dams to be classified as "wild" or "scenic," the act does not specifically prohibit consideration or construction of new impoundments. Assumptions are that state designation will guarantee state opposition to dams and that state agencies will become better funded and more capable in solving recreation and resource management problems. State zoning of private lands is not permitted under the law, nor is condemnation of land, though the Commonwealth can use the right of eminent domain to acquire right-of-way easements to the water.

Crossing the pipeline, lower Lehigh Gorge

Year-long studies are being undertaken to determine if the streams should be designated and to draft guidelines for managing the rivers and their adjacent landscapes. A number of issues were to become apparent on the Lehigh Advisory Committee's float trip—a field investigation by people involved in preparation of the Scenic River Study.

In two vans driven by local outfitters, we rumbled down the stony road to Rockport. While this area is acceptable for the commercial operator, it is not recommended for private or individual access—your car will likely be sacked by local residents who have had their fill of floaters. At the bottom of the hill, doors burst open, and a parade of government people and Lehigh enthusiasts poured forth. I was especially anxious to see the river. This was my first visit to the gorge, and I had heard lots of tantalizing stories. Four rafts carried Department of Environmental Resources officials, Fish Commission personnel, county planners, and citizen members of the study committee. Charlie Walbridge, representing the American Canoe Association, and Roger McCay of the Forest Service took a C-1 (decked canoe) and a kayak, dancing circles around our lumbering "rubber ducks." I had very nearly brought my sixteen-and-half-foot open canoe but cautiously followed the advice of some Lehigh experts and left the boat atop my car at the campground. While a lot of people use conventional open canoes in the gorge, many of them foolishly risk losing their boat and maybe more.

After two minutes of cruising, we made the first stop for reasons I could not imagine and then did not believe. "Someone had an idea for a parking lot over here," Katie Gavan said. She worked for DER on the Lehigh study. It didn't take long to conclude that no road went to the potential parking area. "There would have to be a bridge across the river, but don't worry about it," Katie added. "There'll never be enough money to do it, even if it had been possible. Though the Lehigh qualifies for 'scenic' designation, the intent is to manage it as a 'wild' river, which would likely mean opposition to any new crossings."

Access and parking are important problems that the Scenic River Study is addressing. Currently the only major points for putting in or taking out of boats are at White Haven, Lehigh Tannery, and Jim Thorpe, for a minimum trip of about twenty-five difficult miles. Minor points of access are at Rockport, where cars frequently are vandalized, and Drakes Creek, where an obscure dirt road turns into a jeep trail, then stops 200 feet short of the river. Portage under a railroad bridge is required, and that often means wading in the creek. The solutions will be difficult ones; however, with limited access come opportunities for management of recreational use and related problems. Outfitters on the intensively floated Youghiogheny are controlled by the state, but only because embarkation points are on state-owned land. To regulate use of the river, public control of major access points is imperative.

Local outfitters feel that Rockport should be reserved for commercial float trips, since the guides don't have to leave cars and since they can police the area to minimize litter and other problems that make local residents unhappy. Spokesman Ken Powley added, "We recommend the development of the unpopulated Drake's Creek access area for use by private boaters only, where they wouldn't be interfering with the daily lives of local residents." An additional advantage of this plan is that commercial and independent boating traffic would largely be segregated, since White Haven to Rockport would be an easy shuttle for the outfitters, and Drake's Creek to Jim Thorpe would be good for independents. "We have over thirty miles of excellent whitewater rapids," Powley said. "There's no need for everyone to be paddling up each other's backs." Drake's Creek is far from a simple solution, as a four-wheel-drive vehicle is now needed, and to significantly improve the road would be very difficult.

After looking at the "parking" area and the Drake's Creek access, we entered some wilder rapids, and I got to thinking that I did the right thing in leaving my canoe at the campground. I'd be plenty wet by now. Half a dozen times we passed corpses of canoes which had been, no doubt, the pride and joy of enthusiastic owners. It makes a miserable day when you

Overturned kayaker, Lehigh River

wrap a $400 boat around a rock and leave it there to become shredded in
the coming floods. It's also a long walk out of Lehigh Gorge, providing
you're able. Three weeks before, a man had drowned in these rapids. After
swamping his open canoe, the thirty-four-year-old paddler apparently
wedged his foot under a rock while trying to free the pinned boat. After
falling into the water, he was held under by the force of the current. Wise
advice is to stay clear of the Lehigh in your open canoe unless you're an
expert. Better to go by raft, or if you're experienced, by whitewater
(decked) canoe or kayak.

When we stopped for lunch, Bob Steiner of the Fish Commission mentioned that an estimated 1,200 people floated the gorge on the busiest day
of the year. That's an incredibly high figure, but it's easy to see why the
river is popular. For the kayaking enthusiast, the Lehigh is ideal. Like the
Delaware, it's within easy traveling distance of one-fourth of the nation's
people. For the expert canoeist, the Lehigh still presents challenges, and
for the novice in a raft, it's perfect. The big waters of the Cheat River in
West Virginia and the Youghiogheny in Pennsylvania are *too* wild for many
beginners, often leaving them in fright and outright peril. People who have
never cruised whitewater should not begin on the biggest and wildest
rivers, any more than a casual jogger should enter the Boston Marathon.
The Lehigh offers thrills, wildness, and scenery and can be safely run by
any healthy person in a big rubber raft.

It was October, and we didn't see a single fisherman, but as elsewhere on
scenic rivers, there are conflicts between floaters and anglers. Unique to
the Lehigh, the main concern is the release of water from Walters Dam.
For a number of years, the Army Corps of Engineers has been releasing
extra water on the third weekend of July, August, September, and October, creating a high flow that boaters can rely upon and allowing them to
schedule trips accordingly. Fishermen maintain that extra water destroys
invertebrate bottom life that is critical to the food chain. Invertebrates have
been sampled twice after releases, one survey showing a reduction in bottom life; however, recovery was rapid. With inconclusive results, the Corps
continues to release under an agreement with the Fish Commission and the
Department of Environmental Resources. Boaters argue that natural floods
of far greater magnitude don't significantly harm the fishery, and fishermen say the river is being destroyed. The Fish Commission and the Scenic
River Study team are trying to get all the facts that they need to make their
management decisions.

As we floated further down the gorge, the scenery became more and
more spectacular. Remains of the Lehigh Canal could be seen, and then
mountains rose high at Oxbow Bend; rocky outcrops hung all around in a
grandeur unlike any Pennsylvania stream. At Mile-Long Rapids, the river
rolled and roared, pitching us over boulders and haystacks and rinsing gallons of water into the raft. One cannot remain unenthusiastic about the
Lehigh.

Delaware Basin River Sketches

Lackawaxen River

A large Delaware tributary in the northeastern part of Pennsylvania, the Lackawaxen is formed by its West Branch and Van Auken Creek at Prompton village. The upper river is fast and includes two impoundments. Just below Seelysville Dam, a 250-yard rapids drops twenty feet. Honesdale is an old northern industrial village.

Early spring sunshine, Lackawaxen River near Kimbles

Wallenpaupack Creek enters at Hawley, draining Lake Wallenpaupack. With 5,760 acres of water, it's the largest Pocono lake and attracts a heavy tourist trade. Water is clear, and fifty-one miles of shoreline are forested, with cabins and four public camp sites operated by Pennsylvania Power and Light Company, the owners. Though this is a reservoir, it has the attractive appearance of a natural lake and is one of the finest large flat-water canoeing sites in the state. Wallenpaupack's East Branch is a rushing woodland stream that carves through small gorges and drops over an unboatable falls, one mile above the lake.

Below Hawley, the Lackawaxen is at its best and attracts many fishermen. Outstanding scenic areas are near the Kimble Road Bridge and through the rapids that run for five miles above the Delaware confluence. Pennsylvania Power and Light Company's powerhouse for the lake is located above

Lackawaxen River below Kimbles

the Kimble Bridge, causing flows to fluctuate greatly. Releases are not scheduled, making it impossible to predict water levels. The river drops eighteen feet per mile through this reach, becoming even steeper as the Delaware is approached. At medium and high levels, paddlers can run from Hawley, but rapids are a challenging Class II and III.

State Route 590 and smaller roads follow the river but detract little from a rocky beauty of the shoreline. Zane Grey did much writing in the historic hotel at the village of Lackawaxen, where an archaic suspension bridge spans the Delaware.

Shohola Creek and Upper Delaware Tributaries

Though Shohola is only a small stream draining eighty-six square miles, it deserves special attention because of its extraordinary ruggedness and beauty. The creek rises on the high and boggy plateau of the Poconos near

Shohola Falls

Resica Falls, Bushkill Creek

Lords Valley and Greeley, then flows northeast to the Delaware, which it joins at the village of Shohola. Route 6, which many people consider Pennsylvania's most scenic highway, crosses just below Shohola Falls, one of the state's most picturesque cascades. Three hundred yards above the falls, an ancient glacial lake has been reimpounded on state game lands, but at the falls, waters plunge madly over broad sandstone ledges, darkened tannin color contrasting sharply with white aerated foam. Massive, glistening rock outcrops and deep shade of hemlocks all add to the scene. Below the falls, Shohola churns downhill through a gorge that is almost impassable on foot and totally impassable on water except for the most expert kayakers who float during high runoff. Fishing is good, with many anglers at the lake, a few who cast into the deep black pool at the foot of the falls, and rarely anyone in the rugged gorge where pools are much smaller.

Like Shohola, other tributaries to the northern Delaware are small streams, with the exception of the beautiful Lackawaxen. Big and Little Bush Kill are special attractions. On the larger stream, Resica Falls is a highlight that can be seen at the Boy Scout camp along Route 402. Bushkill Falls is a very long drop, located on a private, commercially operated site north of Bushkill village.

Brodhead Creek is also an upper Delaware tributary, well known as an excellent trout stream. Proposals to construct small dams have threatened the Broadhead in recent years, though they have thus far been successfully fought by environmental groups such as Trout Unlimited.

The Schuylkill River

The Schuylkill is best known for its broad reach of flatwater behind Fairmount Dam in Philadelphia. This is a rowing center of the world, and
racing shells can almost always be seen with their crews of one, two, four,
or eight men or women. In 1876, 800 acres were taken from industrial,
residential, and vacant space along the Schuylkill and used for the nation's
Centennial celebration. Two hundred buildings were constructed and later
removed to create Fairmont Park, the largest urban park in the United
States. It includes both sides of the river and lower Wissahickon Creek, a
small tributary with a history of protection activities that has involved many
generations.

Schuylkill water quality has a reputation of being poor. It was long a

Eight-man crew, Schuylkill River and Fairmont Park

joke, and perhaps a fact, that an overturned oarsman should get typhoid shots immediately. The last twenty years have brought improvements. The riverbed and shores were black with coal sludge until much of it was removed in the 1940s. Fish passages are now being built for the ocean-migrating shad at Fairmont Dam and Flat Rock. Wastes from mining have largely been curtailed, but many industrial and municipal problems remain. Swimming is limited indefinitely due to high fecal coliform. Philadelphia draws 180 million gallons of Schuylkill water per day for municipal use. Four other communities tap the lower river for consumption. Increases in power plant cooling and irrigation are projected, with conflicts over appropriation. Water is now utilized six different times before it reaches Fairmont Dam, and by the year 2020, water will be used a minimum of eight or a maximum of sixteen times.

Floating debris, Schuylkill River in Philadelphia

Yet the river is in a strategic place for recreation. It flows through the nation's fourth most populous city, and 28 percent of Pennsylvania's residents live in the five counties that face the waterfront. Some of the river is noxious and carries the noise and cemented banks of industry, like the reach below Norristown Dam. Other areas are fine assets: the scenic Blue Mountain Gap below Port Clinton, the recreational pool above Felix Dam, and the edge of Reading's riverfront park. Philadelphia plans to restore a section of the Schuylkill Canal in the Manayunk section of the city.

Under contract from the state Department of Environmental Resources, the Pennsylvania Environmental Council prepared a recreational river study and a greenway proposal for ninety miles of the river. PEC found that one-third of the riverfront is public or recreational land. The proposal emphasizes establishment of access areas, natural area protection, and the use of special-interest sites, such as the old canal. A Schuylkill River Greenway Association was formed to foster open space and recreational improvement. Importantly, the effort had local political support. Though Pennsylvania has dozens of wilder, more scenic, more open, and cleaner streams than this, the Schuylkill was designated a "recreational" and "modified recreational" river—the first member of the state scenic rivers system. You can't get much closer to the people than this.

The Brandywine and Its Landscape

Brandywine Creek and its resident conservationists have gained special status. Here, in 1945, a group of thirty-five people formed the nation's first major watershed association. Led by Clayton Hoff, the organization sought to eliminate problems of erosion, industrial and municipal water pollution, and flood damage. Their efforts led to substantial success, as 96 percent of industrial waste and 94 percent of sewage wastes are now treated, and soil losses by erosion are reduced by 60 percent. In 1958 the first flood-plain zoning in Pennsylvania was enacted here. The organization supported small dams for recreation, flood control, and low-flow augmentation, maintaining enough water in dry periods so that pollution is diluted and less noticeable. Bob Struble, who headed the association for years, says that their key was to "get people together and work in a quiet, constructive way. Water quality is better now than it's been in one hundred years. Though the process of improvement is slow, we've come a long way."

One effort that didn't go very far was an ambitious proposal for easement acquisition, whereby the Chester County Water Resources Authority would buy certain development rights from landowners of flood plain and steep-sloped areas. The program was developed by the University of Penn-

Brandywine Creek above Lenape

sylvania, the Regional Science Research Institute, the United States Geological Survey, and the Academy of Natural Sciences. Its intention was to prevent environmental damage and to maintain the existing rural character of the upper East Branch. Specialists prepared background materials, information brochures, and, in 1968, "The Brandywine Plan." An introduction stated:

> Urban development is coming to the Brandywine Valley just as it has to neighboring valleys. If this development takes place in flood plains, near streams and on steep slopes, if erosion occurs during construction and sewage pollutes the water, the stream and the general environment of the valley will deteriorate. The purpose of the work currently being undertaken by the Water Resources Authority is to prevent this from happening in the basin of the Upper East Branch by restricting development to areas where it will do the least damage.

For a variety of reasons, the proposals were rejected by most of the local governing bodies. Few residents had any apparent and serious concern that the future would bring problems demanding new approaches to land management. Local organizations were not highly active or supportive, leaving a vacuum to be filled by the Chester County Freeholder's Association, a new group whose goal was to defeat the program. The conflict was similar to many that involve new attitudes about land. As John C. Keene and Ann Louise Strong described it, "Followers of an old way of life . . . confronted proposals that promised change and called for cooperation, a sense of community, and use of governmental power." Condemnation authority was an unfortunate recommendation, serving to fuel fears, arguments, and persuasiveness of opponents. While eminent domain provisions were later dropped, damage had already been done, and many people's minds were not to be changed.

"Too much, too fast, is how I sum it up," explained Struble, who at the time was executive director of the Water Resources Authority and who later ran successfully for county commissioner. "Though the program failed, some of its goals are being achieved by using good conservation practices, local zoning, and easements which are donated to the Brandywine Conservancy for protection as open space."

While efforts at conservation and planning have given notoriety to the Brandywine, the valley is also well known for its history and for artists who have lived there. The sixty-mile-long stream was ideally suited for mill sites, with steep falls and rapids just above Delaware Bay at Wilmington. One hundred thirty-three water-powered industries were in the watershed during the early 1800s. At Chadds Ford the Battle of the Brandywine was fought, British General Howe defeating Washington during the Revolutionary War. The battlefield is now a state park. Many artists have worked and lived along the Brandywine, including the well-known Wyeths. Historic sites can be visited through use of a taped driving tour, produced by the Brandywine Valley Association, the Chester County Library, and the Chester County Tourist Bureau, available at the County Library, 235 West Market Street in West Chester.

For a better view of the stream itself, canoe the Brandywine from Northbrook on the West Branch or from Lenape, below the confluence of the East and West branches, to Chadds Ford. Flow is usually high enough throughout the summer. Waters are quiet with small riffles, but stone rubble from old mill dams sometimes creates short, exciting rapids. Above Wilmington, waters become too rough for boating, with waterfalls, dams, and a 120-foot drop in four miles.

Opposite: Skinner's Falls

Travels on the Delaware:
Whitewater, Herons, and Kids from the Bronx

It was like a festival, and everybody was excited. "There's only *one* of these places," I said to myself as I pulled the Delaware River backward with my paddle, then drifted toward the gravel beach near Skinner's Falls. The kids! There must have been a hundred altogether, and thirty of them hopped around on the shore as impatiently as my labrador retriever when there's something to fetch.

"What's his name?" one of the boys asked.

"Eli," was my answer, and then the dog's torment began.

"Eli! Here, Eli," a twelve-year-old girl squealed, but the black lab stayed put in the bow of my canoe.

That Tuesday afternoon was the highlight of a 130-mile canoe journey. Water roared through the rapids for 100 yards, churning up foam and pulling down canoes of the inexperienced and careless, which seemed like most of them. Wherever water falls, an alluring magic fills the air and electrifies those nearby. I thought of the million-dollar fountain-building industry that strives to create and transport a tiny piece of Skinner's Falls to the center of a shopping mall someplace.

It wasn't just children at the falls; the blend of visitors could have competed with Mardi Gras. Everybody seemed to be represented. The lead

show was a stream of young adventurers who tried their best to float through the whitewater, but some sun-loving local girls also attracted attention. I got out my camera and took pictures of both as Eli and I walked downriver to scout the rapids. Rocks that reached into the water were an anthill of activity—kids on inner tubes would spin with the current, then swim into an eddy and hustle back to do it all over again. Three or four canoes were always being carried upriver so that the Delaware roller-coaster could be run again. Young faces peered out from beneath aluminum boats turned upside down over their heads. Mom and the children had found some shallows in which to swim, and a gang of guys with a radio and a case of beer moved stealthily one rock closer to the girls, who used sunshine to the limits of accepted dress codes. A tourist in a red shirt and blue socks was rolling movies from an outer vantage point. Suddenly he turned to shoot Eli and me as we zigzagged in his direction, up one rock, down another.

Just in time, he took a new bead on the river, aiming his camera for a comic sequence of four guys in an overloaded boat that was headed toward the center of troublesome water. The first big wave splashed over their bow. The second added two more gallons of the Catskills and Poconos, and then the woeful canoe entered a series of four or five haystacks—large standing waves about three feet high. With each roller the boat sank lower into the river until the gunwales could barely be seen. The next wave showed only four men from the chest up. Their craft was sinking irrevocably toward the bottom, but with futility they continued to paddle in unison.

Sunbathing, Skinner's Falls

Below Skinner's Falls

After I had advanced my film for another frame, the paddlers and their possessions were scattered from Pennsylvania to New York on either side of the borderline river. Reassembly looked like a hopeless task.

Actually, the fun should be regarded with deathly seriousness. It's no wonder that two, three, or four people may drown at Skinner's Falls in a year. The next boat through the rapids scared me. Two boys who might have been fourteen years old overturned to the *downstream* side. They splashed through the rapids and were pursued by their own canoe; that is, their canoe was drifting through the rapids *behind* them. It looks as harmless as when the sunken boat is in front of its dislocated operator, but a boat to the rear is infinitely more dangerous. If the waterborne paddler hits a rock, the canoe may in turn hit him, pinning him tightly and possibly with his head underwater. As I watched those children flailing at the river and yelling in frenzy, their 2,000-pound, water-laden Grumman rolled and tumbled, side over side, just behind them. It was a silent, unseen death trap. Like bad etiquette, the problem is recognized only by those who understand it. The boat rumbled as it scraped rocks, moving inevitably and powerfully like the impersonal giants in fairy tales. Before I tell a beginning canoeist which end of the paddle to put in the water, I tell him to fall out on the upstream side if the boat goes under. Somebody should have said that to everyone who went down the Delaware.

After the children drifted into stillwater, I spotted my route through the rapids. With camping gear, $800 worth of camera equipment, and my only canoe for the trip, I wasn't anxious to overdo it. A thrilling descent would be enough, without big chances on swamping or cracking into the hard earth that separated the Delaware's flow. Before we run Skinner's Falls, maybe we should go back to the beginning.

The Delaware always appealed to me, maybe because it's the name given to the eastern Pennsylvania Indians or maybe because I didn't grow up with the river's tidal stench at Philadelphia. I decided to start as far up as the water level would permit. My route would include the section of river being considered for National Scenic River status and the reach that would be flooded by Tocks Island Dam.

On Catskill waters of the East Branch I embarked with Eli. Scenery was magnificent, the water fast and clear. I had never seen so many great blue herons. They would wade in backwater shallows or go soaring off downstream. After beaching on a small island, I took some photographs, Eli fetched sticks out of the river, and I had my first meeting with other canoeists. Scraping and grating they came. Along with the Wisconsin Glacier, their rearranging of the river-bottom landscape must be one of the more profound changes in geologic history.

"How far to Hancock?" one asked in a weary tone of voice, each word a little lower than the one before it. I said I didn't know. "Well, *about* how far?"

"Maybe five miles." He gave me the blankest stare I've seen, the same stare I used to give Mr. Moore in high-school algebra class. I must have demoralized them. I hoped that they didn't get out to hitchhike, since it turned out to be only a mile and a half to town.

We met the West Branch late in the day. In a golden sundown I looked back up at Point Mountain and the confluence of two branches—the beginning of the whole Delaware. A current whipped around the downstream end of an island, and I followed it into a sharp eddy turn. There lay an idyllic site—a high sandy bank with aged pines clustered all around. It was the most beautiful grove I'd see on the entire trip and also the best camp, except for the last night, when we settled upon a wooded bank and looked out at the Delaware through old-time sugar maples above Tocks Island.

Monday morning was misty—a sunny day coming for sure. I like to travel silently in the fog, and so I drifted without effort toward Equinunk, Long Eddy, and Callicoon. The upper reach of the Delaware is one of the most scenic sections. Even though a road sometimes follows the valley, it's rarely seen, nor is its traffic heard. McCoy's Knob and Jensen Hill are high, splendid backdrops to a moving current. Except for smaller trees today, much of the river must look as it did when Indians called it Poutaxat, Makiriskitton, Makarish-Kisten, or Whitiuck.

It is easy to see why the upper Delaware was included in the National Wild and Scenic Rivers System. With designation has come a prohibition against dams, a restriction that could be important someday. Potential res-

Historic Lackawaxen Bridge, Delaware River

ervoir sites are listed at Hankins, Callicoon, Tusten, Hawks Nest, and Skinner's Falls. Federal status is also to result in maintenance of recreation areas and more attention to trash and litter disposal, sewage waste, and other recreation-related problems. In 1977 Representative Peter Kostmayer of Pennsylvania and Senator Clifford Case of New Jersey introduced bills to designate this and middle reaches of the river—action to prevent construction of Tocks Island Dam. The 1978 Parks and Recreation Act finally designated the upper and middle Delaware.

Long Eddy was the first town after lunch. From a picnicking family I sought directions to the village store and permission to use the access area. After buying a pint of ice cream, I returned to the beach and watched the arrival of two vans and canoe trailers. I'd heard there were some big liveries on the river, one with 600 boats and a few others that rent over 200. Pandemonium broke loose, and the picnicking family was inundated with canoes, kayaks, life vests, happy people eager to get on the river, canoe trailers turning around—you name it. I took off downriver and ended up spending much of the afternoon floating along with the fun-loving group that included the lifeguard, canoe rental girl, and stable boy from the Upper Delaware Campground at Callicoon. I asked about people's feelings on National Scenic River designation, which was pending at that time. "Some want it, but they don't want more people coming here. They don't want a dam, either."

One would think that people who take the time, trouble, and expense to canoe our rivers would do so without leaving trash behind, but that isn't always so, as I found out Monday night. The eastern shore looked like a perfect camp site—a sloping beach, a higher wooded bank with sugar maples, and just for extra measure, an evening view of Callicoon and the old seminary that stands high above the town. I was tired and ready to camp, but as I beached I caught a strange odor, the kind that revolts me but excites my labrador retriever. With differing anticipation, we both climbed the bank to see what it was.

I never really figured it out, and neither did the dog, though leaving that place was my choice and a hard thing for him to do. A fire still smouldered, and at least part of the bad odor came from it. The amazing thing was that behind the fire sat half a dozen garbage bags bulging fuller than a stuffed turkey at Thanksgiving. People must have been proud of the care they had taken to put all that trash together and package it so nicely that it would be no problem for the pickup man in the morning.

Awakening on Tuesday morning, I knew it was early, because when I raised my head, Eli didn't raise his. Later a cool gust of heavy mist blew through the mosquito net of the tent door. It's like having your face washed by the morning itself. I didn't know what time it was but didn't care either. Canoe trips allow you to depart from the normal procedure of checking the morning clock. A watch is something I never take; that way I do what I want instead of what I'm supposed to do.

In a leisurely way I prepared breakfast, then we started our journey as sunshine began to penetrate the fog. After paddling half a mile, I turned to inspect the upstream view. It looked like the Spanish Armada coming behind me, in the distance, at the beginning of a long flatwater reach that I was now leaving. I couldn't see them or their boats, only wet blades of paddles flashing silver as the sun struck them. First one boat, then three, and when I turned the next time to look, there must have been twenty. Forty paddles were blinking on and off through the last remnant of mist that clung to the river. It didn't take long for the group to pass us.

At Cochecton, a public access area of the New York Department of Natural Resources attracted me to the shore. This welcome was appreciated after passing so many "no trespassing" signs. With the camera gear over my shoulder and the dog held tightly on a nylon rope, we started off to town for supplies. I tied Eli to a post at the store front, though he was never happy that way—especially here, as a half-pint dog kept yapping at him from the second-story window. I thought I heard Eli say, "You come within three feet of this post and I'll swallow you whole." I went inside.

While the owner was ringing up my three-dollar order, Eli let out a bark that just about shook the jelly jars off the shelf. "There's so many damn dogs in this town I can't keep track of 'em," the man said. I just sort of agreed and got out of there as fast as I could.

When we reached the canoe, I opened my new sandwich. A little kid on

Trash left by campers, Delaware River near Callicoon

a minibike whipped down the bank and onto the gravel bar. "You goin' to Skinner's?" he asked.

"I've already been there." This really set him back. "I'm going *up* the river."

"Without a motor?"

"The dog pulls—see this harness?" I held up my usual tangled mess of rope. He blinked, looked at the dog, and then a big toothy grin spread from one ear to the other. He knew I was joking.

"There's really big waves. You better watch out!" I thanked him as we drifted away, under the bridge. "You better watch out," he repeated. His voice was faint now from the space between us.

Skinner's easier side is on the right, so that is where I ran. I went cautiously, not wanting to ship water or hit any rocks. After standing for a good view, I picked my way around two outcrops of sandstone. The big waves were coming, so I backpaddled to slow the boat, floating up on the first wave, bracing heavily with the paddle so the boat wouldn't sink into the next haystack. The second and third rollers came closely together. To avoid burying the bow in the lower wave, I canted the canoe a little sideways, and we dipped and rolled parallel to the waves, with only a pint of water slurping over the gunwale and onto Eli. I told him it wasn't much, all considered, but he still didn't like it and gave me an indignant look, as if I'd accused him of not being a pure-bred lab. I couldn't tell for sure what was ahead until I stood up again. Hardly any whitewater remained, so just for fun I reached to the left and drew hard, pulling the boat into heavier rapids.

It was then that we hit a flat rock, the kind that lurks a few inches under so that water slicks over them without much evidence. The real danger is beyond, since a minor collision on a flat rock can throw the canoe off course or destroy a sequence of moves intended to guide you past the next obstacle, and the next one and the next one. That's what happened, so I scrambled to go right where I had intended to go left, while I yelled at Eli to sit instead of trying to turn around each time a wave approached from the opposite side. I smiled as we passed the last rock and swung the canoe into an eddy so we could beach. Hearing a yell, I turned to look and saw a dismembered Grumman and crew headed toward me. I picked up a drifting paddle for them while staying clear of the boat, and then we went for a long, cool swim.

We had come only three days down this great eastern river, but already I had seen so much and done so much. The Delaware drifted and plunged and in many ways created or designed all that was around it. Ahead lay Narrowsburg, Shohola and Mongap rapids, the cliffs at Eddy Farm Hotel, a long winding course past Milford to the Tocks Island Dam site, and then the Delaware Water Gap where we would have to stop. Like life, the river changed every minute; each day would bring a new world, and I would leave an old one behind. It's a fascination that seizes me on all trips, especially after the second or third day out—the movement and life that travel *as* a river, and the places and lives *along* the river.

A whole new riverine perspective appears at Narrowsburg. In a strange pattern, the shorelines bulge to a wide, circular basin that is constricted at its lower end in a narrows for which the town was named. Rocks protrude on either bank, supporting a high arched bridge that connects Pennsylvania to New York. After passing under the bridge, waters of the Delaware are again freed of shoreline encumbrances, forming a lakelike basin beneath clustered homes and shops of the small New York town. Rising from the cliffs and partially encompassed by the river, Narrowsburg looks like a medieval fortress, and sure enough, it was a challenge for me to dock my boat and enter the town without wading, sliding, and falling back into the water.

The effort was worthwhile, for Main Street had an unusual small-town charm. While there were excellent river views, the "downtown" area was well above flood levels. Recognizing a happy group of city kids who had passed me a few miles upriver, I got one of them to hold Eli while I ordered a sandwich. The children were staying in town for a movie that night. Their counselor told them the name of the show, and one asked, "You mean there's only *one* theater in town?"

Into the evening I paddled, passing other groups of young people who were having the time of their lives canoeing, camping, swimming, and cooking supper.

One of the finest sections of the Delaware lies below Narrowsburg, though I was able to enjoy it the least since it rained for a half day. Shohola Rapids were my favorite of all. Less celebrated and without the high excitement of Skinner's Falls, they still offer challenging whitewater, particularly to the novice paddler. Boulders are strewn like buckshot, more like the glacial streams of New York and the north than the smoother-bedded rivers of Pennsylvania.

Seldom would I overtake another party, as I enjoy the slower pace of the river and give priority to bird watching, listening to kingfishers and hawks, and just looking around. So it surprised me that I was gaining on a group of eight aluminum canoes that were spread thin from the east shore to the west. Nearing one of the boats, I noticed its unusual crew. In front were two little girls whom I guessed to be in second or third grade. Never before had I seen two people sitting on one canoe seat. Neatly packed gear was piled amidships, and in the stern was a girl who couldn't have been older than fourteen. We began talking, and I learned that Virginia was a camp counselor—in all likelihood the youngest one on the Delaware. Fred, who runs the summer program for the Putnam School of Greenwich, Connecticut, paddled over to get acquainted and then drifted off to check on another one of his boats. With two college students, Fred and Virginia guide six trips each summer for students of all ages.

"My dad taught me how to canoe," Virginia explained, "but not in rapids. I learned that pretty much by myself." We talked about Skinner's Falls, and I explained the dangers of swimming through the rapids with a swamped canoe behind you. "Hey!" she said, getting the attention of the two second-graders. "Did you hear that?" She explained the danger to her crew exactly as I had done, concluding that they should bail out on the upstream side if the boat goes under.

After a while Fred yelled over, "Virginia, get your friend to have lunch with us—I want to talk to him about Pennsylvania rivers," and so we beached at the mouth of a trout stream.

The children fussed over Eli and were impressed with his swimming demonstration. I said that he had webbed feet to help him, which of course they didn't believe. While I held a paw and pointed to the layer of skin that connects a lab's toes, Fred asked about other rivers that he and his students could run. "The Delaware's great, but this is our fifteenth cruise!" I was amazed that he had no rivers to run in New England. "Except for northern Maine, we don't have a single free-flowing stream for a long trip," he explained. "The Delaware is the closest."

I mentioned the Susquehanna above Wilkes-Barre, and the West Branch. "But you won't find the Delaware's rapids," I warned, "and while the upper West Branch is wild and scenic, it's another three hours from Connecticut."

Everyone depended upon Virginia for lunch; while others casually talked and ate, she spread jelly on top of peanut butter over and over again and at the same time passed out fruit and equitably rationed a pile of candy bars. I didn't want to leave, but as the rain started, I did, draping an extra jacket over Eli's back so that he looked like a racehorse who had just won the Kentucky Derby. We joined the current again, and I waved goodby to new friends.

After a few hours of flatwater paddling, we came to rapids where the Mongap River has built a delta and pushed the Delaware against a cement wall of the railroad on the opposite side. Currents are deep and fast, creating haystacks, any two of which could swamp an open canoe. I eased off to the left and then splashed through the lower rapids that lie half a mile below. It was twilight when we approached Cherry Island. Looking into the river, I saw a half-dozen enormous trout and countless fish of other species. It was like an aquarium.

At Cherry Island we floated through more riffles; then as nighttime neared, we entered the long set of rapids below Millrift. This whitewater came unexpectedly. In growing darkness, the force of an unknown river shook me in a way that recurs often enough that I maintain a healthy fear of water. I intended to make camp half an hour before, but all semblance of a reasonable schedule faded as we came upon Eddy Farm Hotel.

One should understand that my reaction at seeing the hotel was influenced by the circumstances: this was the fourth day of a journey through sparsely developed country, and it was the end of a day that seemed to

The Putnam School canoe trip, Delaware River above Mongap

Virginia, paddling the Delaware below Shohola

have begun forty-eight hours earlier. Only twilight remained as I dropped
from rapids into a deep green pool with fern-covered cliffs on the western
shore. First I noticed a boat dock and manicured beach. Sun umbrellas
called to mind scenes of leisure that are atypical of any Pennsylvania river.
Lights shone through dense foliage, and there stood the hotel. The towering wooden frame building seemed to ramble on forever with wings and
dormers and porches. I think that the sounds were the most alluring aspect
of all, for across the quiet waters came laughter and delight, the crisp noise
from glasses and dishes, and occasionally a voice that stood apart from the
rest. Then I saw the style of luxuriant recreation that had been so popular
fifty and eighty years ago in the Catskills, Adirondacks, and at Eagles Mere
above Muncy Creek. A camp site could wait—any poison ivy field would
do. "Let's go take a look," I said to Eli, and so we walked up from the
beach, water seeping from my ragged sneakers.

Delaware fisherman near Port Jervis

First we met an elderly woman with a twinkle in her eye. She fussed over the dog and graciously told me the name of the place. Our inspection of the grounds was uneventful until we reached the shuffleboard courts. A big man with a shiny bald head looked up from a row of chairs he was straightening and said flatly, "Who are *you*?" I told him. "Do you know that this is private property?" I explained that I was canoeing and photographing the Delaware River, and the trip wouldn't be complete if I passed this place by. He liked that.

"We have nothing against *you*, understand; it's just that we have thousands of canoeists passing by, and we have to say 'no' sometime." He ended up saying it was all right for me to return in the morning to take some pictures.

Early on Thursday morning, we reached Matamoras on the Pennsylvania side and Port Jervis in New York. A foul smell rose from the water, and I was happy to keep passing through. Fishermen were all around on the shore and in rowboats. As we cruised under the Interstate 84 bridge, New York ended and New Jersey began.

The Delaware became a lazier river, and the sun appeared in full force, so that I became a lazier paddler, content to lean back in the canoe and close my eyes as we drifted, occasionally splashing cold water or going for a swim to cool off. The slow river was elegant if not exciting, a friendly sea to turn to, a ribbon of life through the palisaded valley that divides New Jersey mountains from the Pocono Plateau. As we floated to the end of Namanock Island, voices broke through the trees. Reaching the downstream point of the island, I saw a dozen canoes and a lot of young girls. Looking closer for a leader, I could find none. The oldest one was about Virginia's age. They had come four days from Lackawaxen and would finish at Dingman's Ferry—a trip of over forty miles. I paddled away, wondering why there weren't more older people traveling and vacationing by canoe; the pleasures of river voyages shouldn't be reserved for the young. In winding corridors everywhere, waterways show open land, public property, and fine scenery. The experience is almost painless, unlike the rigors of backpacking. Floating a river is the only way to really see it and experience its life. Cars are of limited value, since the most beautiful streams are where roads are not, and usually when rivers can be seen from the highway, the view is marred by the road itself. The canoeist almost always has a choice of excellent camp sites and good opportunities to see wildlife. One can view the rivers as a vast public transportation network that penetrates the most beautiful Pennsylvania countrysides, while augmenting instead of detracting from the scenery. Roadside clutter, exhaust fumes, and noise that are created and tolerated in "pleasure driving" are nonexistent. Rivers are the focus and the highlights of our lands, lacing them together in a web of life and serving as an unmatched recreation system.

For some time we had been floating through the thirty-seven-mile section of river that would be flooded by Tocks Island Dam. Authorized by the Flood Control Act of 1962, the project was designed for flood control, water supply, power generation, and recreation. A lack of funds delayed it for ten years, at the end of which the forces of environmentalists and river protectors were gathered. An initial eight-page environmental statement by the Army Corps of Engineers was rejected, and in the course of intensive study that followed, a proposal to use the National Recreational Area without the dam gained favor. By 1975 all the involved states but Pennsylvania opposed the dam and in 1978, National River designation set a congressional barrier. Efforts are now being made to deauthorize the reservoir—an action that would formally reverse Congress's 1962 commitment. Only two projects in the nation have been deauthorized.

The Pennsylvania Department of Environmental Resources maintains that storage is needed for assurance against Delaware Bay salt intrusion, though the state's criteria are far more stringent than federal standards. The middle Delaware's future has been contested for sixteen years, and while the advocates of free flow have won some important rounds, a counterforce may continue for a long time.

After camping on a shaded sugar-maple bank at Wallpack Bend, we drifted in a light drizzle during the last day of our trip. The base of Kittatinny Mountain rose from the east shore, and 1,000 feet above stood the summit, Sunfish Pond, and the Appalachian Trail. While a party of fifteen canoes went past, I beached on Tocks Island and photographed the immense maples and hardwoods crowning fertile lowlands that were built by centuries of silt and sand deposits.

Six miles ahead lay the Water Gap and the towering cliffs that would mark the end of our 130-mile voyage. With changing waters, the traveler himself changes, and I recalled the perceptions and moods that I had met. First was an excitement of traveling and of moving through the current. Then a smooth contentment came again and again with misty mornings, the plunging dive of a kingfisher, afternoon sun, and the shimmering of water late in the day. To this, people were added in a kinship as citizens of the river—a companionship unlike that of neighbors or old acquaintances. All of the travelers seemed to be one collective friend, and the relationship built with each new face. The Delaware's rhythm replaced the routine of my other lives.

Beneath us the current surged up again, casting us further to the south. River traveling had become more than a canoe trip, more than recreation or seeing new lands. The experience suddenly expands beyond its appearance. Drifting in the widening rapids and eddies becomes a way of life as one leaves the common molds and joins the pace of the waterway. For a while I was lost from the other world, insulated by shorelines and mountainsides. We were exploring a continent, and each mile showed us land that we had never seen before. One can do far worse than to spend a lifetime traveling rivers.

Swimming from the canoe, Delaware River above Tocks Island

Above: An urban river — the Susquehanna at Harrisburg

Photo by John Lazenby

Below: Pine Creek below Blackwell

The Future
of Pennsylvania Rivers

Pennsylvania's rivers are a valuable resource, with qualities difficult to find elsewhere. For residents of the valleys and for visitors who canoe, fish, hike, and camp, many of the streams offer wildness, clean water, and outstanding scenery. A person can experience peace in solitude or share with others the companionship of the river.

Streams have also been ravaged, polluted, and dammed. We have progressed in some respects, achieving better sewage treatment, less industrial waste, recovery from mine drainage, enaction of flood-plain regulations, and a program to designate scenic rivers; but most of the problems from the past remain. The early 1970s have shown a net improvement in 670 miles of major streams, but thousands of waterway miles still do not meet established standards. Future changes are likely to place even more stress on certain aspects of the riverine environment. With more people there is more waste.

Leetonia, on Pine Creek's Cedar Run, used to have fifteen hundred people; now it has half a dozen. Without the sawmills and tanneries and boom towns of the nineteenth century, some waters of the north central highlands are cleaner. But the backwoods and rural reaches of Pennsylvania are entering a new era today, growing with urban emigrants. Escapees from cities and suburbs are reversing seventy years of exodus from the countryside, small towns, and quiet villages. People clamor for land. In many mountainous counties they find 95 percent of the soils poorly suited for on-site sewage disposal. The state Department of Environmental Resources had barely finished tightening enforcement to prevent pollution from poorly sited septic tanks when pressure from bankers, developers, and local governments forced a liberalization. "Alternate" disposal techniques, such as sand mounds, now account for half of the new systems in some areas, but over 40 percent of these malfunction and overflow.

Rural Pennsylvania is ill-equipped to cope with the coming tide of popularity. No sewage permit is required by the state if the new owner has ten acres of land. The township can require a permit, but few do. These new settlers can dump wastewater as they please, affecting the environment as much as the owner of half an acre. It makes the difference between drinking and not drinking from many mountain streams.

More graphic is the problem of municipal and industrial disposal, though improvements have been made. The Ohio River, where I grew up, was a sordid conduit of waste that no one thought could be clean. You were considered nostalgic to think about a clear forest-shored Ohio; the river was obviously meant to transport sewage and steaming overflow from the steel mills. It's said to be better now, but far from good. The first time I canoed the Susquehanna's West Branch, sewer gas at Williamsport smelled like a trapless bathroom drain. Today the river is usually green and odorless, with bass and walleye, though some sewage overloads persist. Throughout the state, the job of municipal clean-up is still onerous, and without subsidies from the federal government little will be accomplished. Galeton, in Potter County, can't afford to install adequate sewage treatment, even with 80 percent funding assistance from state and federal agencies. It's a low-income community, bustling only with the invasion of deer hunters and trout fishermen.

Galeton is a small problem; consider the enormity of waste on the lower Delaware, the Schuylkill, the lower Allegheny, the Monongahela, and worst of all, the Mahoning River as it flows down from Youngstown. To reclaim these waters would require fortunes of investment. With scarce financial resources and enforcement personnel, the best approach may be to first eliminate the toxic waste and serious health hazards wherever they occur, then try to keep the clean waters clean. It's a difficult question of priorities. We could reclaim the Schuylkill and gain 100 miles of less polluted water, or we could prevent pollution and correct more minor problems on perhaps 1,000 miles of nonurbanized river.

Some progress has been made with industrial wastes. Eighty percent of industry's treatment plants are reported to be in compliance or satisfactorily working toward requirements, but with 2,200 treatment works and another 2,900 sewage plants in the state, who knows for sure? Corning Glass was credited with a 650 parts per million discharge of fluoride—highly poisonous to life—but the factory is now meeting Department of Environmental Resources regulations. Environmental Hearing Board action was scheduled with Hammermill Paper Company, but improvements are now being instituted at their Lock Haven mill. United States Steel spent $30 million to treat a water discharge near Pittsburgh, but when the question involved air emissions, they responded with attorneys and a long siege of resistance. Bethlehem Steel begged clean-up extensions from the federal Environmental Protection Agency, finally receiving an exemption after the 1977 Johnstown flood, as the company threatened to lay off 7,000 flood-stricken employees. Legislators introduced a bill to fire DER's Deputy Secretary for Enforcement William Eichbaum, who forced reform on many of the state's worst polluters. Big industry is tough, and while the Commonwealth dealt seriously with environmental protection under DER Secretary Goddard and Deputy Eichbaum, there is no guarantee that commitment to clean up the big, well-financed problems will continue.

Nonpoint sources of pollution are some of the most troublesome. These are wastes from large land areas and not from a single discharge. Silt from farmland is the greatest source, such as the suspended soil that makes the Conestoga and other agricultural rivers opaque brown or yellow with mud. Farmers are worried that there will be new, costly controls for things like manure-spreading. "Conservation plans," prepared by the Soil Conservation Service, are now required for erosion control.

Pesticide and herbicide wastes have effects that we aren't even aware of. Most applications of DDT have stopped, and already the osprey and eagle populations in some parts of the nation are increasing. More of these raptors are appearing along Pennsylvania waters. The safety of herbicide 2,4,5-T has been seriously questioned, though it was widely used by the state Department of Transportation in border spraying and by utilities to kill plants along power lines. In 1979, most uses of this poison were banned.

Storm water and runoff from urban areas contributes in ways that individually are imperceptible. Oceanographers estimate there is more oil in the sea from drained crankcases than from wrecked tankers. After high school, when I worked at the wire mill along the Ohio River in Monaca, I'd collect the milky-gray metallic sludge from wire-grinding machines and dump it out the back window of the plant.

Acid mine drainage degrades over 2,000 miles of major streams in Pennsylvania. Old abandoned mines are responsible for much of the problem, a

Industrialized river: the Ohio and J&L Steel at Aliquippa

West Branch Susquehanna above Williamsport

point much touted by today's mining interests, but far from the full truth. In the last sixteen years, ten clean streams between Karthaus and Renovo became polluted, and it was no horse-and-buggy deep mine from 1890 that did it. "Operation Scarlift" has spent $193 million to abate acid and restore land, but the job seems endless. Pennsylvania was long recognized as having the best strip-mine regulations in the nation, but the streams didn't get the message: they're still turning orange and acidic. Enforcement is the problem, as many sites are rarely inspected, and some inspectors have done their job on an "appointment" basis. In recent years stripping activity has increased dramatically. "New mining doesn't mean pollution," it's often said. Believers are plentiful, but evidence is scarce. Cooks Run is a good case: after conservationists protested, a mining permit was issued on the West Branch Susquehanna stream above Renovo. A year later, with two-foot-high grass, the reclamation was said to be exemplary. Then aluminum-polluted groundwater burst out through a spring, decimating life in eight miles of excellent trout water. In another case, the Jersey Shore community water supply is threatened by aluminum from a mine that's been scratched and blasted at the municipal watershed's border.

Clean streams in coal country are scarce and of great value to many people. With demands to get the coal out, the most important approach may be saving the undisturbed watersheds while mining the ones that are already polluted. Wilderness trout streams designated by the Fish Commission and the basins of clean streams where DER has tried to discourage mining include less than 5 percent of Pennsylvania's coal. At current mining rates, there are about 600 years of known coal reserves in Pennsylvania; the clean-stream coal could be saved until the year 2450. Society doesn't need it, but only the owner of the minerals and the miner, who want the money now. Their reasoning sounds identical to that of the rural developer who argues for the right to do whatever he pleases with his land. No matter that the miner doesn't own the land or the trees, the soil and the water. If he owns only the minerals, courts support his right to turn the surface upside down so he can haul his glittering black cargo off to the coal tipple.

Regulations to reserve undisturbed streams are now incorporated in the "conservation stream" classification of the Environmental Quality Board, but custody is very weak. New federal strip-mine regulations call for the protection of clean-stream areas. We need to do the job now.

Power generation bridges the issues of water quality and supply. Thermal pollution has been a problem at electric plants, where the river is heated far beyond natural levels, killing native fishes. To avoid some of this, cooling towers are designed so waste heat goes into the air instead, generating steam and often consuming a significant share of the river. At the extreme are nuclear plants, where excessive heat demands vast amounts of water.

Where does it come from? The natural volume of our streams is limited.
To maintain adequate in-stream flow for other users and for wildlife, regulations have been effected that require the river level to drop no further
than the lowest average consecutive seven-day flow that's likely to occur
once every ten years (Q-7-10). Major consumers, like power plants, will
have to provide "make-up" water—stored water that can replace their cooling water. That will likely mean dams, either private ones or public ones
where the consumers "buy into" the project.

Water supply is becoming more critical than ever before. Per capita consumption is sixty-five gallons per day. Major urban centers face potential
shortages, highlighted in the Monongahela basin. Today New York City
gets water from the neighboring Delaware basin, and the lower Delaware
gets water from the Susquehanna. These "interbasin transfers" may become a major controversy in the future. Will Keating Dam on the wild
canyon of the Susquehanna's West Branch be justified by supplying water
to Philadelphia, 200 miles away? Will Tocks Island Dam on the Delaware
be constructed someday? And what end is there? Pennsylvania proposed
Rowlesburg Dam on the Cheat River in West Virginia. In 1966 the Army
Corps of Engineers identified Barbours, on Loyalsock Creek, as one of the
ten best sites in the state. River protection depends on energy and water
conservation, which can greatly extend our ability to get along without sac-
rificing additional natural streams.

Besides water supply, common objectives of the dam builder are flood
control, hydroelectric production, recreation, wildlife enhancement, and
economic development. These issues have been discussed in the Moshannon and Clarion chapters and others. Without adequate flood-plain management, high-water hazards will only become worse, leading to yet more
river destruction and more flood-plain development in a cycle of ever-
fewer flowing rivers and ever-greater flood disaster potential. Benefit-cost
ratios are used to justify public water-resource projects, but there is a need
to recognize the less tangible costs of forsaking the natural river, and the
broader economic costs of building dams: timber and agricultural yields
that are lost, recreation loss, maintenance through dredging, repair of the
dams, and disposition only one hundred years from now when they become public hazards and monumental white elephants.

Human needs and wants inevitably affect rivers. This book does not
argue for restoration of nature as though people don't exist. Nor does it
argue that our desire for recreational or metaphysical experience should
override demands for food, shelter, and other important goods and services. My plea is for a balance among competing pressures—for responsible
stewardship. Although these chapters criticize special interest groups, I recognize that progress toward environmental quality has been made, and that
there are environmentalists everywhere, including concerned persons
within the industries and agencies that I have criticized.

While pressures mount for the use of rivers, an evolution of attitudes is

Mobile homes on the flood plain, West Branch Susquehanna below Jersey Shore

Flood damage to mobile homes located on the flood plain

another phenomenon we are facing. The commitment of people to maintain the quality of natural rivers continues to grow. In future years many decisions will be made about the waters that have been described in this book. The National Wild and Scenic Rivers System and the Pennsylvania State Scenic Rivers System will likely include some of these streams—Pine Creek, the Lehigh Gorge, and others. Additional rivers such as the Clarion, Upper Allegheny, and West Branch Canyon of the Susquehanna should be studied and designated. National river status provides the most certain protection for free-flowing qualities—to see that dams aren't built. Pennsylvania already has over 600 impoundments of twenty acres or more. State scenic-river status may be the only way to assure a Commonwealth policy of protection for our best remaining streams, and for adequate attention to management of public recreation and the problems that it brings.

A state water plan is being prepared by the Department of Environmental Resources, which could form the basis of many decisions regarding protection and exploitation. The Commonwealth also plans for statewide recreation programs, and the Army Corps of Engineers plans for dams and water-resource developments. Counties and local governments plan for land use, flood plains, and related concerns. All of these programs will have an effect on the future of waters, and nearly all effects will be a result of compromise, determined through some degree of public debate. You can and should be a part of it. Responsible compromise recognizes the needs and desires of the whole citizenry, present and future, and of the limits beyond which important values have been lost. To have all rivers half-polluted or half-dammed would be a loss. Comsumptive needs are not so vast, nor is our thirst so great that we cannot save the best of our free-flowing streams. But even if that were the case, could one find better proof that our society asks for too much?

Knowledge of our rivers and our needs is essential if we are to make the right decisions. Equally important is a consciousness of values to be protected, so that the next generation and all people in the future will enjoy and prosper through an environment that meets our spiritual as well as material needs. Unless people are willing to learn and perceive and protect, the rivers will never again be as wild and scenic, as enjoyable and impressive as they are today.

For months and years I've explored the rivers of Pennsylvania. They've led me to rainy nights, snow-covered mornings, high and muddy waters of a half dozen floods, and a wild exuberance with sunshine and rapids on a hundred afternoons. The rivers run on and on, over and over again in a pattern that has molded a continent. In learning to live with their seasons, to respect their nature, we can guarantee their qualities and their use in the future. The rivers are here for themselves and for us to travel and admire; they are the shining life of our land.

West Branch Susquehanna below Williamsport

Information for River People

Recreation along Pennsylvania Rivers

Fishing, canoeing, rafting, camping, hiking, picnicking, swimming—all these kinds of recreation can be enjoyed along the rivers of Pennsylvania. People are attracted to the freedom of open spaces and the scenery of these flowing streams. As with other liberties, recognition of responsibility is important—to ourselves, to other people, and to the environment.

Safety

We owe ourselves reasonable precautions for safety. Common sense is the most important ingredient. Canoe, kayak, raft, or inner-tube travelers should know how to swim. Meet a person who knows lifesaving techniques for water rescue; they make good paddling partners! Better yet, learn the rescue skills yourself. Techniques in mouth-to-mouth respiration and cardiopulmonary resuscitation may save your best friend's life. An American Red Cross first aid course is a good way to learn these and other lessons. The Red Cross handbook, *First Aid and Emergency Care,* is a reference for most problems.

When you're on the water, wear a life jacket (technically termed a "personal floatation device" or PFD), especially if the water is deep, fast, or cold. The law requires one vest per person in each craft, a rule that should be taken seriously. Fish Commission deputies have inspected my canoe twice. High waters and floods magnify hazards. Quiet riffles become a course of haystack waves and whirlpools. Logs, stumps, and springtime ice can complicate an already vexing current. If there's a chance of extremely high water, investigate conditions before beginning your trip. Never wear hip boots or fisherman's waders in a boat. If the craft capsizes, they fill with water and pull the wearer straight to the bottom. Powerful currents handicap any fast-change artist who tries to escape from his footgear. Don't overextend yourself. Know the difficulty of your water and the level of your personal skill. Ten miles per day is enough for many paddlers, though some may want to go twenty or more.

If your boat has overturned in the current, stay on the *upstream* side of it. The importance of this cannot be overstressed. If you're not upstream, then swim *away* from the boat. Contrary to this warning, many paddlers have been told to stay with the canoe if it capsizes, since it will float. This is

Opposite: Fisherman on Penns Creek below Poe Paddy

flatwater advice; it could cost you your life in the current of a river. Many whitewater fatalities are due to entrapment: the capsized swimmer hits a rock or tree, then his boat hits *him*, pinning him tightly and possibly with his head under water. To fall out on the upstream side should become second nature, like falling backwards when skiing. Don't walk in fast water that is more than knee-deep; a foot can become stuck between two rocks. If the current pushes you over, a broken foot may be the less serious consequence, and your chances of drowning are good. Immediate aid to victims of entrapment is essential but often impossible. Whitewater boaters should see the article titled "Avoiding Entrapment," by Charles Walbridge, in *Canoe* magazine, June 1976.

Hypothermia, when the body loses more heat than it generates, is perhaps the most common and greatest danger of all. Uncontrollable shivering is a sign of danger. Keep dry or get dry; warm up fast. Much is written about hypothermia. For important details, see the editorial in the January 1977 issue of *Wilderness Camping* magazine, or almost any book on canoeing. Springtime is especially dangerous; a person who falls into forty-degree water will be unconscious in fifteen to thirty minutes. Be cautious, and consider wearing a wetsuit when waters are cold.

Except for people with special allergies, biting insects are more of a nuisance than a safety problem. Nonetheless, one should be prepared. In Pennsylvania we're fortunate, being north of most ticks and chiggers and south of the black flies. At certain times we have mosquitoes, no-see-ums,

Youghiogheny, Entrance Rapid

Owassee Rapid, Pine Creek

deer flies, and biting "house" flies, though these are just a mild sampling from boggy bug country in the Adirondacks, Maine, Minnesota, Canada, Alaska, and other lands of the river lover. A good repellent will keep mosquitoes from penetrating. It's best to ignore their nerve-wracking, high-pitched song. No-see-ums have waked me many a night, chomping into the epidermis after climbing through the tent's mosquito net. Until I got a tent with a fine mesh screen, I sweated through summer nights with the nylon door zipped shut to keep the tiny pests out. Deer flies bite like an alligator, only more so. My biggest problems are with the dog. The flies burrow into his fur and send him howling. Aboard ship, a furious eighty-pound labrador retriever is a tough force to reckon with. He becomes determined to catch that fly.

Most concerns about wild animals are remnants of the medieval understanding of the wilderness as a place of mystery and werewolves. Snakebite is about the only valid concern in Pennsylvania. The bite of a rattler or copperhead can cause critical illness, especially in a child. Watch out, particularly when rock climbing, berry picking, or engaging in other activities with your hands or head near the ground. Look where you step. The worst places are where it's rocky, sunny, or near still water in the dry season. Everyone should read first aid instructions regarding snakebite; see the Red Cross manual.

Water pollution, unfortunately, is a safety hazard that cannot be ignored. All but the small, undeveloped, and unmarred tributary streams are too polluted to drink. Coliform bacteria from sewage waste often exceed state standards for swimming, though I've survived many a substandard plunge. Except where toxic wastes may be a problem, most people do well when relying on their senses to determine adequate quality for a summertime dip.

Safety is the individual's responsibility, but other people assume a share. Paddlers have risked their lives in saving their wet companions or strangers. Government agencies have been held accountable for accidents and thus have assumed a paternalistic view on some issues of safety. Requirements regarding equipment, the timing of float trips (such as no cruising in high water or cold weather) swimming, and other facets of the river experience could be expanded to stifling levels. Nobody wants more regulations, but unless the users themselves show the caution necessary for their own safety, the government will be abrogating more and more of the individual's right to travel and play as he pleases.

Recreation Problems

It is ironic that the great movement to enjoy our rivers is creating its own problems. On some streams, the very values that attract people are jeopardized by popularity. With small amounts of recreation, the riverine environment can withstand abuse without showing much strain, but with more activity, high standards of responsible behavior are critical.

Many visitors come to the public lands and mountain rivers of rural Pennsylvania to get away from people, to be alone, or to do things they aren't allowed to do in their crowded home town. The fact is, there *are* people here, and their rights to privacy deserve respect. Before using populated lands for access to a stream, stop and ask permission. There's no sense in creating a bad image or getting shot at. Most owners will say okay if the visitor has the courtesy to inquire.

In heavily used areas, local residents accumulate a common list of complaints: fishermen park in front of driveways, and trespassers roam about or camp without permission. On the Delaware, canoeists stop to ride a farmer's horses! The less inhibited visitors will change clothes in front of homes, and there is always the sewage problem. Worst and most prevalent is trash and litter. Visitors should take their trash home. Never bury it at camp sites; frost or raccoons will bring it to the surface. Many people have the idea that garbage collection at any access area is someone's responsibility. Usually that isn't the case. Some outfitters and landowners haul trash from publicly used sites, which is most generous of them. Some public sites are maintained, such as Fish Commission access areas, but these are rare or nonexistent on smaller streams. As for the person who throws his soda bottle, beer can, or plastic tackle wrappings along the stream, to break a Norse paddle or an Orvis fly rod on his head would be worth the cost and the risk of aggravated assault charges.

As much as we seek solitude, experiences on rivers in Pennsylvania are usually social to some degree. To be alone, I run rivers on weekdays, especially in the spring. Most often we're sharing the stream with people, and a respect for their wishes is important. Boaters should try to avoid fishermen and to pass them quietly. Motorized recreational vehicles are usually offensive to everyone but the user of them. People who are seeking to escape urban problems and a pervasive gasoline-powered technology take no pleasure in more exhaust fumes, noise, and abuse of trails or fragile landscapes. All wild-country visitors should be as inconspicuous as they possibly can.

Our touch on the land need not be a heavy one, weighted with change and the increasing spread of trash and noise. Concern for safety, environmental quality, and the rights of other people can lead to recreational activity that serves important needs without degrading the resource or other people's experience.

There are many places to go. Most streams are specialists offering particular values, and recreational visits should be planned accordingly. Consideration of travel time, safety, visitor facilities, and degree of remoteness may be important to any outing. All recreational opportunities cannot be listed here. The intent is to present selected highlights that are only an introduction to thousands of waterway miles.

Canoe camping, upper Susquehanna

Camping and General Recreation

Pennsylvania state parks provide many opportunities for picnicking, camping, swimming, fishing, and stream access. Rustic riverfront cabins are available for rent at several state parks, including Clear Creek on the Clarion and Worlds End on the Loyalsock. Reservations must be made in advance with the Department of Environmental Resources, Bureau of State Parks. For more information, write to the Department of Environmental Resources, Bureau of Parks, P.O. Box 1467, Harrisburg, PA 17120.

Other riverine recreation facilities are located in Allegheny National Forest and the Delaware Water Gap National Recreation Area. Many state forests offer public land for hiking, stream-side camping, and fishing. Public access areas are provided along some rivers by the Pennsylvania Fish Commission. The maps in this book show the location of public lands, parks, and access areas.

Many private campgrounds can be found along the rivers, such as several large sites along the upper Delaware and Allegheny. For information on private recreation establishments, write to the Pennsylvania Bureau of Travel Development, Box X, South Office Building, Harrisburg, PA 17120, or the chamber of commerce of any county or large town.

Hiking

While there are hundreds of trails on public lands in Pennsylvania, they generally do not follow a major waterway for any great distance. Several trails parallel rivers for short distances, offering outstanding hiking experiences and excellent scenery. A few favorites include:

Slippery Rock Creek at McConnell's Mill State Park.

Clarion River at Cook Forest State Park.

Spring Creek, a tributary to the Clarion in Allegheny National Forest. Old railroad grades are rough but can be hiked, and trout fishing is good.

Youghiogheny River at Ohiopyle State Park. Short but unusually scenic trails lead to the river from Cucumber Falls and Ferncliff Park.

Grove Run, a small stream in Linn Run State Park.

Hammersley Fork of Kettle Creek, a small but wild stream in Susquehannock State Forest. The Susquehannock Trail is eighty-five miles long and includes the Hammersley. Hiking is best done as an overnight backpack trip. For trail maps, write to the Susquehannock Trail Club, Susquehannock Lodge, Ulysses, PA 16948.

Pine Creek at Colton and Harrison Point State Parks. The Turkey Path and Four Mile Run Trail wind precipitously from canyon rims to the valley floor. These trails are especially hazardous in early spring and should be avoided until the ice melts.

Loyalsock Creek, accessible from the Loyalsock Trail, which runs southwest from Route 220 near Laporte. The northernmost two miles parallel the creek, leading to the rugged Haystack Rapids.

Penns Creek, where an old railroad grade can be hiked for eight miles, accessible at Weikert or one-half mile south of Coburn.

Schrader Branch of Towanda Creek, a small stream that can be followed along an abandoned railroad grade on state game lands, beginning near Wheelerville. Fishing is excellent.

Kitchen Creek in Ricketts Glen State Park, west of Wilkes-Barre. Thirty-three waterfalls range from 6 to 100 feet in height. Many people feel this is the most scenic hike in Pennsylvania.

Schuylkill River and Wissahickon Creek in Fairmount Park, Philadelphia. Paths and bike trails are plentiful and uncommonly pleasant for a major urban area.

Hiking across the Hammersley Fork of Kettle Creek

Many other short hiking trails can be discovered along hundreds of streams. Detailed information regarding trails is available from the Pennsylvania Bureau of Forestry, P.O. Box 1467, Harrisburg, PA 17120, or the Pennsylvania Bureau of Travel Development, South Office Building, Box X, Harrisburg, PA 17120. United States Geological Survey maps also show hundreds of trails. Many require bushwhacking but lead to excellent river views, camp sites, and fishing streams. A useful guide to trails in the central part of the state is Tom Thwaites, *Fifty Hikes in Central Pennsylvania.*

Fishing
Fish can be caught in nearly all Pennsylvania waterways, except those with mine acid* and the most polluted streams near major urban areas. Many of the accessible streams are stocked by the Pennsylvania Fish Commission, which has also developed access areas. Fishermen are notably reticent about their favorite streams, so if you want to know about the really good places, better ask a friend who's willing to share, or just start casting. While cold-water or trout fishing is often more popular than warm-water, Pennsylvania has six times as many acres of warm-water fishery as cold (including lakes). A few of the best and most-used waterways are the following:

Allegheny River from Kinzua Dam to East Brady for bass and walleye.

Clarion River above the town of Clarion. This stream is now improving after years of unrestrained pollution. The West Branch of the Clarion, above Johnsonburg, has always been good trout water.

Youghiogheny from Confluence to Connellsville, another river that has improved greatly in recent years.

First Fork Sinnemahoning Creek, a favorite trout stream that is crowded with anglers early in the season. Driftwood Branch is also becoming a good fishery.

West Branch Susquehanna River from Williamsport to Sunbury. This waterway was affected by mine drainage as recently as 1970, but now offers good walleye and bass fishing.

Susquehanna River from New York state to Scranton. This is a large river with excellent warm-water fishing.

Upper Kettle Creek, Penns Creek, and the lower Loyalsock—all good trout fisheries in the northern and central areas.

Juniata River. Warm-water fishing is good almost anywhere, but especially in the lower reaches.

---

*Coal mining has resulted in the pollution of over 3,000 miles of waterways in Pennsylvania.

Yellow Breeches Creek, an excellent limestone stream popular among trout fishermen.

Delaware River from Hancock to Easton. Don't look for solitude on weekends—there are many, many canoes.

Lackawaxen River, a large tributary to the Delaware.

Other streams are also heavily used. Hundreds of cold, wooded waterways are a prime habitat of the small native brook trout. For the angler who wants to get away from the crowds, these are the places to go.

A fishing license is required for anyone over twelve years of age. Creel limits, seasons, and other regulations must be strictly followed. In "Fish-for-Fun" areas, trout fishing is allowed year round, under special regulations that vary from stream to stream. For more information, write to the Pennsylvania Fish Commission, P.O. Box 1673, Harrisburg, PA 17120. Pamphlets on fishing locations are available, with county maps that show stocked streams. See the map inside the back cover for further information.

River Traveling
People enjoy canoeing, kayaking, and rafting on many Pennsylvania streams. The popularity of river traveling and whitewater cruising has increased greatly in recent years and is likely to continue. The map inside the front cover identifies selected streams and indicates their degree of difficulty. Canoeing guidebooks offer detail on access sites, whitewater difficulty ratings, lengths of various reaches, and other information. Guides can be very helpful, but all river travelers should beware of hazards that may not be discussed in the books or indicated on our map. Owassee Rapids in the Pine Creek Canyon is not mentioned in Burmeister's guide, yet it is significant, dangerous, and unexpected, lying two miles south of Ansonia. Paddlers should consult the following:

Canoeing Guide to Western Pennsylvania and Northern West Virginia
Pittsburgh Council of American Youth Hostels, Inc.
6300 Fifth Ave.
Pittsburgh, PA 15232

Appalachian Waters 1: The Delaware and Its Tributaries
Walter F. Burmeister
Appalachian Books
Oakton, VA 22124

Appalachian Waters 3: The Susquehanna River and Its Tributaries
Walter F. Burmeister
Appalachian Books
Oakton, VA 22124

Select Rivers of Central Pennsylvania
Penn State Outing Club
4 Intramural Building
University Park, PA 16802

A short brochure, which includes major canoeing streams of Pennsylvania, is "Canoe Country Pennsylvania Style," available from the Pennsylvania Bureau of Travel Development, Box X, South Office Building, Harrisburg, PA 17120. Due to low water levels, only a limited number of rivers can normally be floated in the summertime:

Allegheny River, which always has sufficient flow from Warren down.

Youghiogheny River from Confluence down, including many Class IV rapids below the Ohiopyle Falls, which can't be run. Only experts should attempt to canoe or kayak below the falls. Inexperienced paddlers should travel in a raft with a guided party.

The Monongahela and Ohio rivers, though they are dammed, polluted, and developed, more suited for motorboats than canoes.

The West Branch Susquehanna, from Lock Haven to Sunbury. Water volume is usually adequate from Karthaus (between Renovo and Clearfield), though in dry periods the river will require some wading.

Susquehanna River from the New York border down.

Juniata River from Huntingdon down. One difficult rapids is below Newton-Hamilton.

Lehigh River, a whitewater stream where releases from Walters Dam are sometimes planned for the third weekend of each summer month. At other times during the summer, flow is usually not sufficient for floating. For water level information, call the Army Corps of Engineers, (717) 443-9493. The Lehigh is a difficult and dangerous river. Inexperienced paddlers should cruise by raft, preferably with a guide.

Brandywine Creek, from Lenape to Chadds Ford. Old mill dams create short and sudden rapids.

Delaware River, though dry periods will require wading through shallows in northern reaches. Here and on the upper West Branch of the Susquehanna, it's best to plan summer trips for the month of June. The Delaware has some difficult Class II rapids.

Scores of medium-sized streams are excellent for springtime floating or for canoeing after heavy rains. The guidebooks already mentioned list most of these. Some of the finest waters are Tionesta Creek, the Clarion River, Casselman River, Bennett and Driftwood branches of the Sinnemahoning, Moshannon Creek, the upper West Branch of the Susquehanna, Pine Creek, Loyalsock Creek, and Tunkhannock Creek. Intermediate paddling skills are needed for these.

Whitewater streams that offer excitement and challenge to the experienced boater include Slippery Rock Creek, the Youghiogheny River, the Pine Creek Canyon, Little Pine Creek, upper Loyalsock Creek, Schrader

Branch Towanda Creek, Wills Creek, Stony Creek (near Johnstown), Lehigh River Gorge, Lackawaxen River, and some sections of the Delaware. The Slippery Rock, Youghiogheny, upper Loyalsock, Lehigh Gorge, Wills Creek, and Stony Creek are the most significant and difficult of these; only true experts should attempt them in canoes. Two outstanding rafting rivers are the Youghiogheny at Ohiopyle and the Lehigh River Gorge.

Kayakers, Youghiogheny below Ohiopyle

River Rating System
For Whitewater Difficulty

Degree of rapids and whitewater difficulty is expressed in "grade" or "class" ratings of I through VI, developed in Europe and known as the International Scale. It is not a perfect system, but does much toward simplifying and standardizing a river description. Water levels often change the condition of rapids, usually making them more difficult, but not always. Flow characteristics also change from year to year: gravel bars and boulders are rearranged by high water, and trees fall into streams, creating new hazards. While the classification can help in planning a river trip, never rely totally on the books. If there are big rapids, look for yourself before paddling through. The following description is taken from the American Whitewater Affiliation's safety code:

Class I   Moving water with a few riffles and small waves. Few or no obstructions.

Class II   Easy rapids with waves up to 3 feet, and wide, clear channels that are obvious without scouting. Some maneuvering is required.

Class III   Rapids with high, irregular waves often capable of swamping an open canoe. Narrow passages that often require complex maneuvering. May require scouting from shore.

Class IV   Long, difficult rapids with constricted passages that often require precise maneuvering in very turbulent waters. Scouting from shore is often necessary, and conditions make rescue difficult. Generally not possible for open canoes. Boaters in covered canoes and kayaks should be able to Eskimo roll.

Class V   Extremely difficult, long, and very violent rapids with highly congested routes which nearly always must be scouted from shore. Rescue conditions are difficult and there is significant hazard to life in event of a mishap. Ability to Eskimo roll is essential for kayaks and canoes.

Class VI   Difficulties of Class V carried to the extreme of navigability. Nearly impossible and very dangerous. For teams of experts only, after close study and with all precautions taken.

Major Stream Basins of Pennsylvania*

Stream	Square Miles in Watershed
DELAWARE RIVER BASIN	
Delaware River including Lackawaxen River	2,626
Delaware River including Brodhead Creek	4,717
Delaware River including Lehigh River	6,085
Delaware River at Pennsylvania-Delaware state boundary	10,370
Lackawaxen River	597
Wallenpaupack Creek	228
Bush Kill	158
Brodhead Creek	287
McMichaels Creek	113
Lehigh River	1,368
Tobyhanna Creek	128
Pohopoco Creek	111
Little Lehigh Creek	190
Tohickon Creek	112
Neshaminy Creek	232
Schuylkill River	1,912
Little Schuylkill River	137
Maiden Creek	216
Tulpehocken Creek	219
Perkiomen Creek	362
Brandywine Creek to Christina River in Delaware	304
West Branch Brandywine Creek	135
East Branch Brandywine Creek	124
SUSQUEHANNA RIVER BASIN	
Susquehanna River including Chemung River	7,528
Susquehanna River including Lackawanna River	9,887
Susquehanna River at West Branch (but not including West Branch)	11,302
Susquehanna River and West Branch	18,257
Susquehanna River including Juniata River	23,091
Susquehanna River at Maryland state boundary	27,132
Tioga River	461
Crooked Creek	132
Cowanesque Creek	300
Cayuta Creek	140
Chemung River	2,595
Sugar Creek	190
Towanda Creek	278

*Figures indicate watersheds 100 square miles or more, including neighboring states' areas that drain into Pennsylvania. Tributaries are indented.

Source: Pennsylvania Gazetteer of Streams

Codorus Creek	278
South Branch Codorus Creek	117
Chickies Creek	126
Conestoga Creek	477
Cocalico Creek	140
Pequea Creek	154
Muddy Creek	138
Octoraro Creek	176

POTOMAC RIVER BASIN
(figures include area in Maryland)

Wills Creek	194
Tonoloway Creek	112
Licking Creek	189
Conococheague Creek	503
West Branch Conococheague Creek	199
Antietam Creek	113
Monocacy River	240

GENESEE RIVER BASIN

Genesee River at Pennsylvania-New York boundary	136

OHIO RIVER BASIN

Ohio River including Little Beaver Creek	23,487
Allegheny River including Potato Creek	603
Allegheny River including Sandy Creek	6,433
Allegheny River including Clarion River	8,937
Allegheny River at Ohio River	11,748
Potato Creek	224
Oswayo Creek	195
Tunungwant Creek	139
Kinzua Creek	182
Conewango Creek	898
Brokenstraw Creek	329
Tionesta Creek	474
Oil Creek	318
Conneaut Outlet	101
French Creek	1,232
Sugar Creek	167
East Sandy Creek	103
Sandy Creek	161
Clarion River	1,252
East Branch Clarion River	108
Little Toby Creek	126
Redbank Creek	573
Sandy Lick Creek	229
Mahoning Creek	425
Little Mahoning Creek	113

Crooked Creek	292
Kiskiminetas River	1,887
Conemaugh River	1,372
Stony Creek	467
Little Conemaugh River	190
Blacklick Creek	418
Two Lick Creek	192
Loyalhanna Creek	299
Buffalo Creek	171
Monongahela River	7,384
Cheat River	1,422
Dunkard Creek	235
Tenmile Creek	338
South Fork Tenmile Creek	199
Redstone Creek	109
Youghiogheny River	1,763
Casselman River	590
Laurel Hill Creek	125
Indian Creek	125
Sewickley Creek	168
Turtle Creek	148
Chartiers Creek	277
Beaver River	3,153
Mahoning River	1,140
Shenango River	1,062
Little Shenango River	109
Pymatuning Creek	171
Neshannock Creek	242
Connoquenessing Creek	838
Slippery Rock Creek	408
Wolf Creek	101
Raccoon Creek	184
Little Beaver Creek	503
North Fork Little Beaver Creek	193
Buffalo Creek	114
Wheeling Creek	164
LAKE ERIE BASIN	543
Conneaut Creek	152

Recommended Streams (High-Priority Candidates) for Pennsylvania Scenic River Study*

Stream Name	Location

DELAWARE BASIN

Brandywine Creek — Chester, Delaware counties
  East Branch Brandywine Creek
  West Branch Brandywine Creek
Bush Kill (Big Bushkill Creek) — Monroe, Pike counties
Delaware River — Bucks, Monroe, Northampton, Pike, Wayne counties

Lehigh River — Carbon, Luzerne counties
  Glen Onoko Falls
  Jeans Run
  Mud Run
Schuylkill River — Berks, Chester, Montgomery, Philadelphia counties

French Creek — Chester, Berks counties
  South Branch French Creek
Tohickon Creek — Bucks County
Bushkill Creek — Northampton County
Cooks Creek — Bucks County
Jordan Creek — Lehigh County
Lehigh River — Carbon, Lehigh, Northampton counties

Maiden Creek — Berks County
Perkiomen Creek — Montgomery County
Wissahickon Creek — Montgomery, Philadelphia counties

SUSQUEHANNA BASIN

Beech Creek — Centre, Clinton counties
Black Moshannon Creek — Centre County
Hammersley Fork — Clinton, Potter counties
Juniata River — Huntingdon, Mifflin counties
Laurel Run — Perry County
Lick Run — Clinton County
Loyalsock Creek — Lycoming, Sullivan counties
Moshannon Creek — Centre, Clearfield counties
Mosquito Creek — Cameron, Clearfield counties
Muddy Creek — York County
Octoraro Creek — Chester, Lancaster counties
  East Branch Octoraro Creek

*Compiled by the Pennsylvania Scenic Rivers Task Force, Department of Environmental Resources

West Branch Octoraro Creek
Stewart Run
Penns Creek   Centre, Mifflin, Snyder,
                                               Union counties

Pine Creek   Lycoming, Tioga counties
Schrader Creek   Bradford, Sullivan counties
Sinnemahoning Creek   Cameron, Clinton counties
   Driftwood Branch Sinnemahoning
   Creek
Spruce Creek   Huntingdon County
   Little Juniata River
Stony Creek   Dauphin, Lebanon counties
Susquehanna River   Bradford, Lackawanna,
                                               Luzerne, Wyoming counties
Susquehanna River   Dauphin, Juniata, North-
                                               umberland, Perry, Snyder
                                               counties
Tuscarora Creek   Huntingdon, Juniata counties
West Branch Susquehanna River   Centre, Clearfield, Clinton
                                               counties

OHIO BASIN

Allegheny River   Clarion, Forest, Venango,
                                               Warren counties

Brokenstraw Creek   Erie, Warren counties
Casselman River   Somerset County
Clarion River   Clarion, Elk, Forest,
                                               Jefferson counties
French Creek   Crawford, Elk, Mercer
   Cussewago Creek   counties
   Muddy Creek
   South Branch French Creek
   Sugar Creek
     Lake Creek
   West Branch French Creek
Kinzua Creek   McKean County
Laurel Hill Creek   Somerset County
North Fork Redbank Creek   Jefferson County
Slippery Rock Creek   Butler, Lawrence counties
   Connoquenessing Creek
Squaw Run   Allegheny County
Tionesta Creek   Forest, McKean, Warren
   East Branch Tionesta Creek   counties
Wolf Creek   Butler, Mercer counties
Youghiogheny River   Fayette, Somerset,
   Cucumber Run   Westmoreland counties
   Dunbar Creek
   Indian Creek
   Jonathan Run
   Meadow Run
Bear Creek   Elk County

Buffalo Creek	Armstrong, Butler counties
Buffalo Creek	Washington County
Dutch Fork	
Dunkard Fork Wheeling Creek	Greene County
Enlow Fork Wheeling Creek	Greene County
Oil Creek	Crawford, Venango counties
Youghiogheny River	Fayette, Westmoreland counties
Allegheny River	McKean County
Allegheny River	Allegheny, Armstrong, Clarion counties
Aunt Clara Fork Kings Creek	Washington County
Connoquenessing Creek	Beaver, Butler, Lawrence counties
North Fork Little Beaver Creek	Beaver, Lawrence counties
Youghiogheny River	Allegheny, Westmoreland counties

Selected Bibliography

Allen, Barry, and Haefele, Mina Hamilton. *In Defense of Rivers: A Citizen's Workbook.* Stillwater, N.J.: Delaware Valley Conservation Association, 1976.

American Youth Hostels, Pittsburgh Council. *Canoeing Guide to Western Pennsylvania and Northern West Virginia.* Pittsburgh: Pittsburgh Council, American Youth Hostels, 1975.

Amos, William H. *The Infinite River.* New York: Ballantine, 1970.

Banta, R.E. *The Ohio.* New York: Rinehart, 1949.

Beak Consultants. *Wild and Scenic River Survey, Physiographic Provinces 8D & 8E,* vol. 1. Atlanta, Ga.: United States Department of the Interior, Bureau of Outdoor Recreation, January 1976.

Bradford, Willard. *Pennsylvania Geology Summarized.* Pennsylvania Department of Environmental Resources, 1973.

Burmeister, Walter F. *Appalachian Waters 1: The Delaware River and Its Tributaries.* Oakton, Va.: Appalachian Books.

Burmeister, Walter F. *Appalachian Waters 3: The Susquehanna River and Its Tributaries.* Oakton, Va.: Appalachian Books, 1975.

Canby, Henry Seidel. *The Brandywine.* New York: Rinehart, 1941.

Carmer, Carl-Lamson. *The Susquehanna.* New York: Rinehart, 1955.

Chester County Water Resources Authority. *The Brandywine: A Place for Man/A Place for Nature.* West Chester, Pa.: Chester County Water Resources Authority, 1967.

Clement, Thomas M. Jr.; Lopez, Glen; and Mountain, Pamela T. *Engineering a Victory for Our Environment: A Citizen's Guide to the U.S. Army Corps of Engineers.* San Francisco: Sierra Club, 1973.

Directory of Canadian Biography, Volume 1. Toronto: University of Toronto Press, 1966.

Erdman, Kimball S., and Weigman, Paul G. *Preliminary List of Natural Areas in Pennsylvania.* Pittsburgh: Western Pennsylvania Conservancy, 1974.

Fletcher, Peter W. *Man in the Ecology of a Mountain Stream.* University Park: Pennsylvania State University, College of Agriculture, 1971.

Frank, O. Lynn. *80 Miles of Wilderness Adventure on the West Branch of the Susquehanna River.* Clearfield, Pa.: Clearfield District, Bucktail Council, Boy Scouts of America, 1970.

Hornberger, Marlin L. *A Geological, Chemical and Biological Survey of the Effects of Land Use on Little Pine Creek, Lycoming County, Pa.* University Park: A report sponsored by the National Science Foundation and The Pennsylvania State University, 1971.

Kauffman, John M. *Flow East: A Look at Our Eastern Rivers.* New York: McGraw-Hill, 1973.

Keene, John C., and Strong, Ann Louise. "The Brandywine Plan." *American Institute of Planners Journal* (January 1970), 50–58.

Likens, Gene E. "Acid Precipitation." *Chemical and Engineering News* (22 November 1976).

Myers, Barry Lee, Esquire; Bumgarner, Harry L.; and Shirey, Elizabeth G. *Legal Problems Associated with Planning Land Uses in a Riverine Area, Pine Creek, Pennsylvania.* University Park: A report of the Center for the Study of Environmental Policy, The Pennsylvania State University, March 1973.

Naturalist, volume 16, no. 3, 1965.

Northern Environmental Council. *Preservation of Wild and Scenic Rivers from Overuse and Deterioration*. Ashland, Wis.: Northern Environmental Council, 1973.

Outdoor World. *Rivers of North America*. Waukesha, Wis.: Outdoor World, 1973.

Palmer, Timothy T. *Pine Creek, A Summary of Reports*. Harrisburg: Lycoming County Planning Commission and the Pennsylvania Department of Environmental Resources, 1975.

Palmer, Timothy T. *Pine Creek Tomorrow*. Harrisburg: Lycoming County Planning Commission and the Pennsylvania Department of Environmental Resources, 1974.

Palmer, Timothy T. *Recreation on a Wild and Scenic River: Pine Creek*. Harrisburg: Lycoming County Planning Commission and the Pennsylvania Department of Environmental Resources, 1974.

Palmer, Timothy T. *Susquehanna Waterway, The West Branch in Lycoming County*. Williamsport, Pa.: Lycoming County Planning Commission, June 1975.

Pennsylvania Department of Environmental Resources. *Programs and Planning for the Management of the Water Resources of Pennsylvania*. Harrisburg: Pennsylvania Department of Environmental Resources, November 1971.

Pennsylvania Department of Environmental Resources and United States Department of the Interior, Bureau of Outdoor Recreation. *Northeast Regional States Scenic Rivers Planning Workshop: Summary of Proceedings*. Philadelphia: United States Department of the Interior, Bureau of Outdoor Recreation, 1976.

Pennsylvania Department of Forests and Waters. *Outdoor Recreation Horizons*. Harrisburg: Pennsylvania Department of Forests and Waters, 1970.

Pennsylvania Department of Forests and Waters. *Water Resources Bulletin No. 6, Pennsylvania Gazetteer of Streams, Part 1*. Harrisburg: Pennsylvania Department of Forests and Waters, December 1970.

Pennsylvania Fish Commission. *Fishing in Pennsylvania*. Harrisburg: Pennsylvania Fish Commission, n.d.

Pennsylvania Governor's Office of State Planning and Development. *Pennsylvania's Recreation Plan: Summary*. Harrisburg: Pennsylvania Governor's Office of State Planning and Development, March 1976.

Pennsylvania State Planning Board. *Pennsylvania's Regions: A Survey of the Commonwealth*. Harrisburg: Pennsylvania State Planning Board, 1967.

Pennsylvania Wild and Scenic Rivers Task Force. *Pennsylvania Scenic Rivers Inventory*. Harrisburg: Pennsylvania Department of Environmental Resources, 1975.

Power, John, and Brown, Jeremy. *The Fisherman's Handbook*. New York: Charles Scribner's Sons, 1972.

Pringle, Laurence. *Wild River*. New York: J.B. Lippincott, 1975.

Riviere, Bill. *Pole, Paddle and Portage: A Complete Guide to Canoeing*. New York: Van Nostrand Reinhold, 1969.

Schaefer, Thomas G. *Technical Report No. 5: Management Alternatives for the Importance of Canoeing Opportunities and the Resolution of Problems Relating to the Recreational Use of Rivers*. Ohio Department of Natural Resources, May 1975.

SEDA Council of Governments. *SEDA-COG Regional Flood Recovery Plan* (draft). Lewisburg, Pa.: SEDA Council of Governments, 1975.

Susquehanna River Basin Commission. *Comprehensive Plan for Management and Development of the Water Resources of the Susquehanna River Basin*. Mechanicsburg, Pa.: Susquehanna River Basin Commission, December 1973.

Susquehanna River Basin Study Coordinating Committee. *Susquehanna River Basin Study Summary*. Susquehanna River Basin Study Coordinating Committee, 1970.

U.S. Army Corps of Engineers. *Acid Mine Drainage Abatement Program for the Clarion River Basin, Pa.* July 1976.

U.S. Army Corps of Engineers. *Development of Water Resources in Appalachia*. Part III Project Analysis, volume 9, chapter 2. November 1969.

U.S. Army Corps of Engineers. *Environmental Statement: Lock Haven Flood Protection Project, West Branch Susquehanna River and Bald Eagle Creek, Pa.* October 1974.

U.S. Army Corps of Engineers. *A Vacationscape for Appalachia: A Comprehensive Out-*

door Recreation Study of North Central Pennsylvania. Washington, D.C.: U.S. Government Printing Office, 1968.

U.S. Army Corps of Engineers. *Water Resources Development in Pennsylvania*. Washington, D.C.: U.S. Government Printing Office, 1975.

U.S. Congress. *Wild and Scenic Rivers Act as Amended Through Public Law 93-621*. 3 January 1975.

U.S. Department of the Interior, Bureau of Outdoor Recreation. *Clarion River Study: The National Wild and Scenic Rivers Act*. Philadelphia: U.S. Department of the Interior, Bureau of Outdoor Recreation, May 1971.

U.S. Department of the Interior, Bureau of Outdoor Recreation. *The Lower Allegheny River Study*. Philadelphia: U.S. Department of the Interior, Bureau of Outdoor Recreation, April 1973.

U.S. Department of the Interior, Bureau of Outdoor Recreation. *Pine Creek: A Wild and Scenic River Study*. Philadelphia: U.S. Department of the Interior, Bureau of Outdoor Recreation, November 1975.

U.S. Department of the Interior, Bureau of Outdoor Recreation. *Preliminary Environmental Statement: Proposed Pine Creek National Scenic River*. Philadelphia: U.S. Department of the Interior, Bureau of Outdoor Recreation, 1975.

U.S. Department of the Interior, Bureau of Outdoor Recreation. *A Survey of Rivers in the Ridge and Valley Physiographic Province*. Philadelphia: U.S. Department of the Interior, Bureau of Outdoor Recreation, 1976.

U.S. Department of the Interior, Bureau of Outdoor Recreation. *The Upper Delaware: A Wild and Scenic River Study*. Philadelphia: U.S. Department of the Interior, Bureau of Outdoor Recreation, December 1973.

U.S. Department of the Interior, Bureau of Outdoor Recreation. *The Youghiogheny Wild and Scenic River Study*. Philadelphia: U.S. Department of the Interior, Bureau of Outdoor Recreation, 1977.

U.S. Department of the Interior, Fish and Wildlife Service. *Allegheny River Survey: Final Report, August 1, 1969 to April 30, 1975*. Washington, D.C.: U.S. Government Printing Office, 1975.

U.S. Environmental Protection Agency. *Cooperative Mine Drainage Study: Selected Areas in the Clarion River Basin*. June 1971.

U.S. Forest Service, North Central Forest Experiment Station. *Proceedings: River Recreation Management and Research Symposium*. January 24–27, 1977.

Way, Frederick. *The Allegheny*. New York: Farrar and Rinehart, 1942.

White, Gilbert. *Strategies of American Water Management*. Ann Arbor: University of Michigan Press, 1969.

Wildes, Harry Emerson. *The Delaware*. New York: Farrar and Rinehart, 1940.

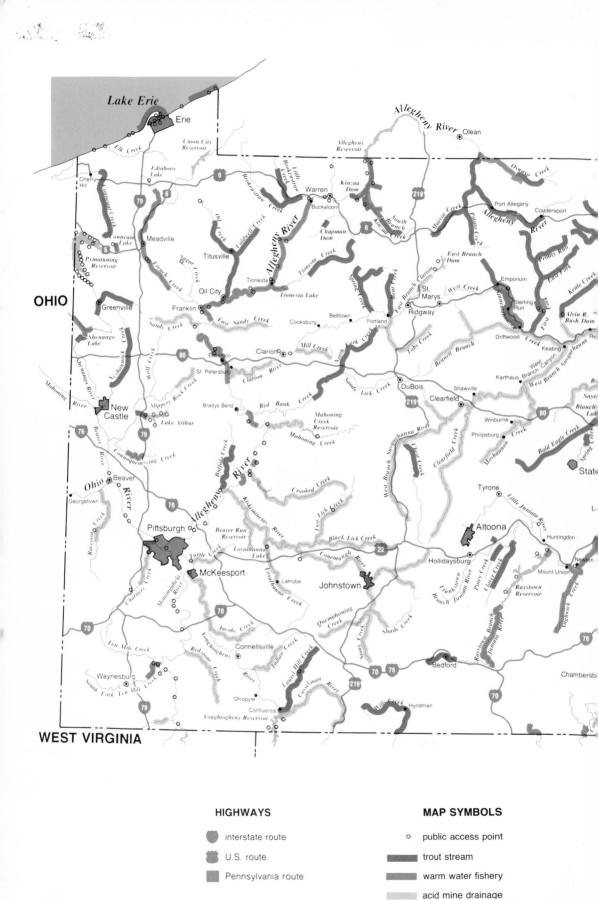

Lake Erie

Erie

OHIO

WEST VIRGINIA

HIGHWAYS

- interstate route
- U.S. route
- Pennsylvania route

MAP SYMBOLS

- ○ public access point
- trout stream
- warm water fishery
- acid mine drainage